RED LIP GIRL

Ricardo Lawton

Red Lip Girl by Ricardo Lawton
ISBN- 9798334743076
Published by Independent VoYces Literary Works a division of Tallawah Inc. Panama
Cover designed in Canva by Judith Falloon-Reid
Printed in the United States of America by Amazon Kindle Direct.

CONTENTS

LOVE & FAMILY

The 'Odda' Mother/Not Our Fault

Through all these years we have grown to understand,
The memory of a woman, who gave up her own,
All those minutes when I had those curses inside,
Concealing all those prisoners that were intricately denied.

Mother! Today is your special day.
But the words I love you is very hard to say.
Mothers! The nations seem to say.
Thank you for staying through the thin-thick gold trail days.

All those years we sat and discussed,
The endless pains of feeling a mother's true love,
Could this determine a better direction or not!
Always remember these situations were created especially for you.

Through all those years we laughed and chatted.
Making pretensions about the day she would appear,
And the way how we would react,
Would this be easy as the way we dressed?
Or would it be the pseudo-communication between the living and the dead?

Mother! Try to always remember this before resting.
You were especially needed in the very tender stage of pure insecurity,
I may not talk a lot in your presence, but avoid mental distortions.
Please remember I have developed and learnt to wear this personality type suit.

There were times the thoughts appeared to
commit suicide.
LORD! There were days the volcanic eruption
caused a bleeding inside.
Ouch! The mother sickness popped up today
and had to be screened away.
My companions! Please remember the
situation was not our fault.

Red Lip Girl

You create this heat in my world.
Constantly rechecking your every mood,
You with your rosy and astounding look,
Your pages I would unfold to understand your book.

Red lip girl I am day dreaming, I am walking, I am talking.
Red lip girl you got me moving, you got me groaning, and you got me moaning.
This minute I am screaming, heart is melting,
When you lifted this cold spirit of mine!

That very day I can remember when you gave me your signal.
You were standing, I was staring, and oh you were daring!
We were whetting, hearts were beating when the fire started.
Red lip attraction, total satisfaction from our reactions,

The sweet and natural glows of your red lip energizes me;
Makes me want to touch you, makes me want to love you.
To always be around you, gets me shaky, acting kind a freaky.
You taught me how to uncomplicate my burdens.

This Love Of Ours Will Last

Truly this day our hearts will be one.
It came the day you asked, and you won.
This is the moment we'll treasure.
My love and your love can't be measured.

This love of ours will last.
Forever and ever, we'll remember to do our part.
You and I are cemented from the heart.
In this love of ours that will last.

Tenderly we'll stroll along the aisles.
Smiling faces and cheers are on each side.
With this ring on our fingers and a kiss so mild,
Always we'll remember to do our part.

Hand in hand we'll move towards the door.
Loving each other as we walk across the floor.
This night I'll make you cry for more.
As we dine, make love and explore.

The Game

She said, "Time I don't need another broken heart".
He said, "Time I'll show you that love can never part".
Oh Lord! This time you cheated and deceived me from the start.
Please understand! Cos' love grows on and on like the grass.

She said, "Love your dishonesty was like a dagger to my heart".
This time love! You weren't there to shed my lonely tear.
I'm always there! For you to play and quench your thirst,
Blatantly no! It would never happen if you were there.

Why can't you speak the truth? You're the special one in my heart,
Love! Wholehearted you are always my number one.
Get to your point! I have grown to understand all your play.
Why can't you believe! Is it the easiest thing for a man to say?

Life's Circadian Rhythms

The simple things we often neglect will be the
revolutionary factor which haunts for life.
Friends we often take for granted we'll lose forever
one day.
And family members we often discard emotionally,
Will upset our body's sophisticated internal clock.

Time and barriers separate us from saying goodbye
in special ways;
To individuals who have strummed their life's drum in
compassionate circadian rhythms.
Daily in our life until that questioner pause comes.
The longing for, the loneliness will linger on in
The twilight of the heart when the beloved is gone.

Inez Richert

She came to light at an early age.
Great and small were in the audience that attended her acts.
She performed on stage.
The dream girl who was my number one,

Many said things I didn't like.
A man in love sees wrong as right.
A fool in love with her picture is far out of sight.
Love with your brain and never your heart.

When I heard you got married tears came to my eyes.
This is the moment a man will cry.
Love is the scissors that cuts my heart.
Some men will not express they're feeling because they are shy.

Why did I forsake the love I had?
In place of her picture she could not stand.
Dreams and reality is a damn hard thing.
Getting in love is like a nuclear bomb.

Inez Richert I knew one day we'll meet.
You were a superstar to those on the street.
I gave my heart and this made me so weak.
My Mona Lisa who was so unique

Full Attention

Today you left me without a speech.
In my heart I cried for one last plea.
I knew it was wrong to be playing all along.
Oh Lord! It's the same old me with the same old plea,

I will never be unfaithful.
Oh babe! Why was I so ungrateful?
Please try to understand you deserve my full
attention.

Remembering the times when love binds.
We stuck with each other in all that matters.
I recall your whispers and our unhappy times.
In retrospect it was easy to say.

In This Relationship

In this relationship we need time.
Please let's free ourselves to understand this uncomplicated life.
It's a mystery to find two lovers at war.
Cursing and fighting in places like bar.

In this relationship let's open and share.
All this need is a little concern to love and care.
My feelings and your feelings, oh my dear!
Are precious like jewels in a glass ware.

Don't frown or worry when I'm with a girl.
You're my beautiful petal on a flower which makes a whirl.
Can't you understand that you are my number one?
Please don't fry me like a fish in saucepan.

Unplanned

We've known each other for years,
We've been through blessings and tears.
Oh babe! It's hard to estimate the angle we made.
I prayed nightly to make this life unchanged.
How it started to God it's uncertain.

To love is unplanned.
To caress and kiss increase tensions.
To rid this feeling, we approach using love making.
Love is a doing thing, not only a feeling.

Could there be a pin in my heart?
Which sticks the minute your presence is not felt?
Would you use feelings to calculate it?
Would it be purposeful to measure these hits?

Please don't leave! It's hard to cry.
How do I cry when the pain has blackened inside.
It would have been better to have died
Rather to be covered with this blackness inside.

Science of Love

To you my love is cohesive.
In my heart, when I see another it gets adhesive.
When I am getting lonely your love can bury.
Whenever you are near it gives birth.

With the science of love the conditions are:
Sensitive, caring, intimate; erotic, non-committal,
captious, and empty
What of being in love is dreaming?
The why of being in love is seeking?

The when of falling in love is provoking?
The where of falling in love is motivating?
The how of falling within love is bodily speaking?
This orchestra is the science of love.

I gave my all for nothing
My dreams were shattered the day your love ended
In another your love was embedded.
Oh yes! My feelings were strong, but my perceptions
wrong.

There are opportunities to take.
Heartaches we must forsake.
Frictions to be mended and gravity to make it
blended.
Marriage is for surety and divorce for insecurity.

With the science of love,
we learn to live not live to learn.
There we experiment in loving to live,
never living to love.
Loves origin is sweet,

but with the passing of time it may become stale.
In this phase of hate by the weird of the wild!

One Earth, One Life

Funny how this life can be,
The ones we love are often neglected.
When they are gone forever a part of us seems to die.
Their absences cause our laughter to turn to unhappy sighs which haunts for life.

One earth, one life, let's get together and change our style.
Do we need to cry to show you these signs?
Heads of government are helpless in distributing the wealth of their nations quite even.
The world moans as the massive die through poverty, diseases, and war torn paths.

It's a shame to see families separating.
Parents are fighting while children are crying.
It's a hell of experience to be suffering.
Life on earth is slowly going.
Humans cravings create this massive dying.
This portrait is sad but is indeed heartbreaking.

The B Constitution

When it mattered the most you didn't care,
Where it mattered the most you were never there,
Your lies and pretensions were disguised in your crocodile tears.
It's risky relating to a woman whose interest lies only in money and material, oh dear!

He gave so little, but you loved him so much.
The one you depended on to be your provider never existed as you were out of touch.
In the community you made it known, he was the prominent figurine to dress your heart.
Has the invisible walked the street, the lonely forsaken brat?

Your attitude dictates that my obligation was for finance, his has been for romance.
A friend of mine retorted "a man never feeds at only one mouth".
Like a remora that feeds on its host so this insensitive consumed with utter disgust.
Love's sunshine provides nurturing to some plants;
It burns others to death through drought.

The planets revolve around the sun with varying degrees of velocity.
Your orbits and tilted attractions were held in place by gravity.
Love and hearsay behave somewhat like fire.
They germinate slowly, consume rapidly like news then fade as a new cycle begins.
Real love stipulates death in this compromise.
It made you soar as my world crumble in crisis.

As our love dissolved our presence could be felt like tension in a high powered wire.
Our eyes reveal the crude bitterness that engulfs our hearts,
As we relate in an air of pretension consuming like an angry fire.
Love under the influence of hatred and bitterness can drive a compulsive lover to kill.
The body dies as love subsides in a similar way like pain is tranquilized by a pill.

Mahogany

I always knew then every woman has her attitude.
I also knew every woman loves the limelight and the glamour of romance in the night.
There are many women who treat men wrong when they are treated right.
They like to travel the globe to know the degrees of longitude and latitude.

I never knew what it was like to be treated as a fool.
My good nature you abused by hammering me with your attitude.
Dear little princess! You want a man to show you love and a heart of gratitude.
Gosh! Please don't treat your man the way you discard your tool.

Those petty plays and positions we take; I love the way you navigate.
These treasured memories I can't forsake, ecstasy is your destiny.
Our hearts beat faster when we see each other, creates a tingling burning sensation.
It's the feelings, the tensions and frictions that occur when we touch the private section.

I become eager and pace the floor with lots of hesitation and desperation.
The head recedes with pictures when you are anchored on this mahogany.
I am so mesmerized by your elated rides and the melodious ahs of your sighs.
It makes you hum like the bee; real love subsides as it flows from the labia major.

Overwhelmed

Girl, I admit the things I've said and done were wrong.
I knew I should have stayed instead of walking away.
I never knew that losing you would make me cry.
This is the moment I put my pride aside; I need you precious gem in my life.

I walk the street not knowing where to go.
You were the purpose that made my life flow.
I'm mesmerized even in my bed about the lovely times we had then.
I find it hard to sleep, I am so distressed every hour of the day I think of you.

I am leaning at the door contemplating home as no meaning anymore.
I am in a vacant place where you were the main feature on every floor.
Girl, I told you I'd never need you in my life, I know now it's a lie.
Sincerely I apologize on my knees, this heart has died like those who commit suicide.

I'm overwhelmed by this continued darkness in my life.
Love! I can't pretend I'm overshadowed by this drought eating my inside.
Day and night I whisper on the phone for you to heal this hurt but there's no insight.
Girl no other love can replace these empty feelings I experience every night.

Love's Global Positioning System

If I should search the world,
I wouldn't be able to find another like you.
All the gold and silver can't be compared to you my greatest treasure.
You bring meaning to my life; you are like a buried treasure I discovered.

Your mom was the bow, she released you, the arrow that captures my heart,
No chasm can separate this love; it glows continually as a star.
Daily I pray and whisper to our Creator to safeguard you everywhere.
This heart grows fonder; it keeps track of you by operating as a global positioning system to know where you are.

Every page I read reflects this book which captivates my heart.
Each day brings hope of a new chapter to face life storm.
You are the moon that brightens the horizon of my path.
What we do and share shows love more than what you say.

French Wine

I left work with the intention of reaching home.
I met this attractive lady as I entered the bus.
I stood at the place where she sat, then in a few
minutes we started to discuss.
I asked her, "Why the language of love is always
associated with French overtones?"
We came off the bus where she suggested to abode
at her place.

When she opened the door we began to touch.
Our bodies beaming in motion when I removed her
brassiere,
There my eyes met her bust.
It becomes difficult to swallow saliva when my body is
bursting with gust.
I continued French kissing while removing her Italian
designer clothes.

I was surprised and awed by the designer French cut.
Why the language of love is overtoned with French
touch?
Here I enjoyed her sophisticated and exquisite French
wine.
With lots of ramifications I surely enjoyed her
exquisite French wine.
Our bodies beaming with love as we touch and
petting deeply in French kiss.

I am honey roasted, amused and mesmerized by her
French styles.
I am a Jamaican who enjoys her many positions of
her exquisite French wine.
This wine is contagious but is not a disease;

It is relaxing and keeps you at dis-ease.
It's an exotic brand officially recommended by the French man,
The president of France Nicolas Sarkozy
The doctor says "Viagra is for the impotent but French wine the stimulant makes you rise to the occasion".
It is both a liqueur and an hors d'oeuvre
To appease the erotic art of the human condition.

Intricate

Every time I see you I hold my breath
you are intricate, intricate.
Every time you talk your voice resonate in my head
you are intricate, intricate.
Every time I dream of you I reminisce
you are intricate, intricate.
Every time you smile and say you love me I get
refreshed
you are intricate, intricate.

I was blown away the other day my heart had an
eruption.
My body had an adrenaline rush that permeates my
being. I'm robust!
Pressures, tensions create this heat; no thermometer
can measure this temperature.
This pulsating body invites yours to this nostalgic
place for both a fiesta and reception.

Girl your touch and rides flows sweetly like
Beethoven's 9th symphony.
In my life you hold a place where it is delicate and
sensitive.
Whenever we touch it makes you shake, tremble as
you reach the heavens of ecstasy.
Love should always build and climax like a movie's
cliffhanger, not end abruptly.

Unforgiving

When we started you were at the spring of your life.
Your temperament was punctuated with deceptions
and lies.
My heart you punctured with that frozen look in your
eyes.
I always pondered what was behind that Mona Lisa
smile.

It's unforgiving for love to become a business
associate, and a piggybacking friend.
Your pretentious portrait will end one day in suicidal
death.
It's unforgiving to create fallacious story lines.
All your unfulfilled promises will break the
untrustworthy in self reflection.

The Air Supply soundtrack plays as I contemplate if I
should call you once again.
Then here again I become cautious of your
dramaturgical analysis.
It is the ostentatious presentation of self on the
world stage.
Is it the performance of being bogged down at your
girl friend's place?
Will it be the hasty rush to fix your nails or to braid
your hair?

Do you comprehend in loving one achieves
acceptance as the other bears rejection?
The lucky ones at the receiving end of this continuum
bubbles in self ego, pride, status.
For the unlucky it is frustration, bitterness;

a vivid imagination of what should have been.
The paradox of love is like the pragmatic behaviour of the mysterious sea.

Love's Credit Crunch

I'm writing this note with not many words to say.
There are no pretensions in the immaculate lies we live.
It's pointless, directionless facing cold fronts in the joys of summer.
With innumerable inflations and overloads love crashes in a gigantic credit crunch!

I contemplate, contemplate this is only bitterness and emptiness.
There are no words to explain only hearts and eyes battling this avalanche.
Silence is a deadly weapon in loves down turn in this credit crunch.
You are like the banker, I am the mortgager
the feelings we house faces foreclosure.

Here we are staring at each other face to face.
This is no time for talking, no eye contact only staring deeply in empty space.
Destinies dissolved in this last moment as our eyes are surrounded by this watery gaze.
There is nothing to converse but hurting hearts expressed in facial bitterness.

We had our boom then now we face our bust.
Indefinite silence and puzzled look; it's impossible to communicate through this fire wall.
I contemplate, contemplate silence and stagflation is my greatest distress.
With fiery minds and broken hearts we end this painful chapter of our lives.

Sweetest Extreme

We are staring at each other so daringly.
Two hearts anticipating making contact so indiscreetly.
It's this vivid imagination to explore your body contour artistically.
Love imagined being fulfilled goes to the sweetest extremes.

I review the mind frame of the day we had our first contact.
You were sitting on the grayish stone while washing your clothes.
I uttered jokingly the request for you to wash my back.
Love's sweetest extremes occur as our bodies beam in positions so close.

A day without you makes me rather upset.
Dialing your number only leaves me with this one regret.
The face to face contact we have talking jokes and engaging in this sweating fiesta.
In this intimate world of ours you are the focal point of my centre stage.

A laptop touch can initiate the body's erotic response.
A whisper in candle light environment enhances our body's background music.
An innocent kiss can open and disperse our moods in this bliss.
Two bodies gripped pulsating the rhythms, exploring inside to the sweetest extremes.

Cauldron of Sacrifice

We had the ideals for the foundation of trust.
Girl perceptions are nonexistent if there is no commitment.
I say commitment is the puzzle unraveled in the social contents of sacrifice.
Love matures gradually in death of self as two becomes one.

When we love each other our history merges into one.
You accept my social genetic tree that is deeply embedded in me.
Of thee I accept the parental linage of thy cultural tree.
Love understands and unites our social contents in this cauldron of sacrifice.

Can we compromise in this crisis when it hurts and tears our sacred hearts?
Can we get along in silence with no pretensions in the heat of life's soap opera?
Do we advertise life's drama for observations in our neighbourhood cinema?
We live and learn to accept our social content in this cauldron of sacrifice.

Can you analyze the sensual feelings in this touch?
Can we be cheerful and greet each other politely in the depths of this seriousness.
We should never sabotage, stop loving, enjoying each other in the turbulent weather.
Love develops to acknowledge the dragging of the plug in this cauldron of sacrifice.

Love's True Intensity

This union should remain firm like an evergreen in the snow.
True love anchors deeply like a cactus to withstand the conditions of the desert.
Tarantulas and rattlesnakes will strike with the deadliest venom. Wow!
Love glows with powerful intensity if we remain in this from year to year.

It tears the heart as it trickles down the cheek.
What use is platinum, a diamond or gold ring when we live like wrestlers in a ring?
What's the purpose of rainbow without water droplets, the easterly position of the sun?
Love's core radiates with such intensity in aches of wormwood taste.

It's the graceful appeal to be devoted after the tumultuous chapter of each storm.
The doldrums may be weighing in; love anchored remains in the turbulent up thrust.
We search for love in places, observing people beautiful features and cold characters.
Love's web unites a family on deep divide of political and religious affairs.

The Captivated Persona

Girl, I swear that I could live without you.
Forever you have captivated my heart with your warm persona.
I thought that I could remove you from my heart.
I am always awestruck when your bubbles burst and refresh love anew.

It's not the conversation we have but it's the intimate silence we share.
No one can sever what we have in our hearts.
The loving eye contact, the holding of hands and smiles makes me feel special.
A million kisses from a friend in a special place drifts me beyond space on any day.

Love's tension increases when we seek to build bridges in finding ourselves.
We relate to each other as companions when we treat each other as equals.
True love finds solutions to problems instead of bickering immaturely at each other.
Being with you has brought hope, perspective and a better outlook.

Love Colourize To Terrorize

You colourized his life with love as you terrorized mine.
He was the Earth springing with life; I was frozen Pluto lost and unknown.
You nourished him from your oasis I had to withstand the heat in this desert.
I was the blessing in your life; like a curse you hovered over mine.

A man may stand tall like a castle tower.
He cries ferociously from the inside to conceal all the hurt and pain in life.
Girl, a man may be strong physically, emotionally he is fragile like a glass.
Stolen waters colourize a known lover and terrorize with pain your once true desire.

She is colourized when you withhold exposing her life's diary.
She is colourized when she achieves status to be someone in life.
I am terrorized as love left me erupting in hatred, anger and strife.
I am terrorized as years of lingering loneliness left me bitter and fragmented.

As I behold you, this tension in my body language constantly sticks with pain.
She holds you in high regard but finds it hard to face you.
What is left of love is muscular stiffness and wounds the nurse cannot dress.

This is the condition of the heart
Love colourize to terrorize.

Love's morbid medication constantly subtracts my sleep.
On some days it slows me down to feel helpless like a baby that creeps.
Wow! Today I tried to shake off this stigma; I will not be stained by love's ink.
This world needs thinkers who can do things not doers who do not think.

The Drug Love

Perhaps you are aware of this addictive drug called love.
The very first experience makes you crave for more.
The mind is blown beyond the ecstasy of space in mega thrills.
Day and night the body desires high drives of its passionate effects and chills.

Perhaps you are aware of the universal use of this drug.
Some users contemplate and salivate heavily for its sensual touch.
Others sweat profusely and experience inhibitive body reactions as they blush.
A fiery flame of bodies in locomotion does explode without combustion.

It's the status measurement of manhood in womanhood,
Frankly, it is the sustainer and appetizer for those who are homesick.
The side effects include over anxiety, jealously, severe heartbreaks and death.
Lonely hearts experience disillusion as others exhilarate in compassionate mood.

This drug colours culture but could be the sedative in solving religious tensions.
Imagine what life would be like if it was the first and last resort in home-global tensions.
Love is an attractive scene to most but a few

understand its venom is a deadly weapon.
In density and scope love is genuine in truth and genuine in deception.

Love is for Life

Girl there's not much to say.
You gave up on me because I wasn't going your way.
Babe I won't be the one to ask you to stay.
If you decide to go away,

Love is for life in what we do and say.
Lovers must respect each other until the close of play.
Through good times and bad times from the vows we take.
This decision must be kept until the end of our days.

She found another who didn't care.
Praying and hoping that her type will appear.
In reality very often a lady's fantasies disappear.
For no human is perfect to match her checklist of qualities.

We searched and searched and couldn't find our match.
Our carelessness had caused this mishap.
Sometimes it is better to wait than to hitch hop.
Because love develops slowly like a child,

From our bad tides we did recover.
Trying to rebuild our broken tower,
So spread the news on radio waves.
We'll be getting married today.

Bedroom Maestro

The contents of your heart are spoken through the rhythmic motion of your wind.
This heart is bursting with admiration for your damn physique.
You sure know how to roll those gluteus maximus with those dainty steps.
The dial on my body surely moves with accuracy with the beating of my heart.

You are a refreshing fountain pouring out nature's beauty.
Girl navigate, rotate put me on the floor, bedroom maestro.
We gyrate, anticipate but your next move in those positions are unpredictable.
Are these colourful sensuous touches kaleidoscope of your love?

This is the moment the passions of our bodies are riddle with joy in Egmont Overtures.
Love's tensions erect thy breasts, echoed in thy moans as the clitoris yearns for more.
We change the pace in these fascinating grooves as we alternate to dictate.
Emotions are compact like the compressions in a spring as we orchestrate to facilitate.

Allegro con Brio

Allegro con Brio my compassion craves thy passion of fruition memory.
I'm fondled with provocation to be seduced by thy enlightened beauty.
Purest melody unfolds with contrasting tensions in rhythmic harmony.
Beethoven must have been mystified by a woman's body ensemble.
Dearest love this heart is filled with erotic emotions for thee.
Words sometimes cannot fully express the feelings love unleashes in degree.
Two bodies pour out provocative contents it can no longer contain.

Love's compulsive drives yearn to experience thy Martian ice.
Thy love unleashes the stomp movements splendidly to unlock Erotica.
The language of love blends harmoniously from our bodies' orchestra.
The heartland of thy body's musical symmetry rekindles the soul's chemistry.
I am beauty filled within, thy boundless pleasure of erotic drama.
Thy notes are strummed in perfect timing as grandeur subsides in creative charisma.
Allegro con Brio burst with radiating power as the sun's intensity such sweet serenity.

Heart's Empty Continuum

This heart cries when it's missing you.
Can I stand the pain of being used?
When I'm ignored it's difficult to do normal work anymore.
I feel so ashamed to face my friends, I opt to remain indoor.

Tears may not trickle from my eyes but I'm dying inside.
She drifts my heart along an empty continuum.
I'm dialing a few friends for their advice,
The contents of my heart are portrayed through my eyes.

Can I endure these overwhelming pains today?
My friends instruct me to nail this stake.
This heart knows you were once a really good friend.
Hearts empty of love gradually traps like quicksand.

The heavy contents of our hearts will not whisper in vain.
We face each other as if we are from distant past.
Can we embrace each other with these severe pains?
We glance at each other but our hearts sinks in an empty continuum.

Girl this heart yearns to be fondled by you.

My heart drags along this empty continuum.
I try conversing with other friends; it feels like the space in a vacuum.
This heart will try to screen you out as it moves along.

Sea Hole Blues

Girl, will you ever know the pain I hold in not having you?
I can still recall the ache it took to walk away.
I could no longer live in the shadow as a fool.
The pictures of you unfold like I am reading your book.

Where the drama began and ended burns my heart with pain.
Yet still this heart would like to see just one glimpse of you.
I learnt beyond every sorrow there's a glimmer of hope.
Not every foundation on a mountain is a solid place.

I guessed I built on the area where the blow hole lies underground.
The pressure of air from nature forced the foundation to cave in.
This is the collapsing crisis I faced the day I walked away.
The current of air and water flows to and fro from the land to the sea.

In the turbulent weather the blow hole cries as it sucks things in.
I was devastated from this phenomenon of your sea hole blues.
Some humans are like sea holes; constantly bringing trouble in your life.
You'll have no peace with your friends; the heart is frequently broken.

You know she's not in love with you
regularly she whispers fallacious news.
She's unaware of what your day is like as she spares
only a few minutes with you.
When she's around her conversations is about money
and glamours to buy.
There's a part of me that yearns for you yet I avoid
with remorse those sea hole blues.

Wounded Soldier

I never knew the pains from love could wound so
deep.
To be forsaken of your love girl makes me feel like
weep.
These excruciating feelings become harder to bear
like someone facing shame.
The lady you proclaim to love was only playing game.
I feel like a wounded soldier on love's battlefield.
I'm longing and yearning to desire this lady's love.
This feels like a trap, the lady uses her body to make
me weak.

I've achieved nothing in this crossfire so I know its'
time to leave.
We never had a fight our tongue got loose when we
faced our disappointments.
I'm a wounded soldier who had to bear love's vicious
cycle from year to year.
I'm a wounded soldier bearing love's post traumatic
stress disorder with fear.
Love's wound makes me grieve; surely sorrows
tainted with sweetness are containment.
I'm torn inside and weakened from love's bullet in this
fiery battle in heat.
I'm a wounded soldier who has experienced love's
fracas with defeat.

My Proposition

For thousand of years in all languages love's token is
a special celebration.
Whether rich or poor, love breaks all barriers that
divide a nation,
In this world our love knows no boundary, a well
spring from the heart.
Our love will last forever like this pair of unbroken
circles we'll wear.

When I made my proposition I knew it would come
through.
I had only one objective the moment I saw you.
My testament today before this gathering is to com-
mit my life in truth.
Angels sigh, mothers weep for joy when we say I do.

The words of the Creator are sacred truths; this vow
we can't break.
When we say I do all of the angels will rejoice and
sing.
Heaven knows we were made for each other like this
pair of unbroken circles we'll wear.
You complete me in this testimony with our rings we'll
be faithful and true.

True love is not just a ceremony; it unfolds in the life
we live.
Can we be trustworthy friends forever when we say I
do?
The flames of our love will burn forever in this
testament of our vows.
In this priceless celebration our lives will be the
timeless chapters for all to read.

Young Lover

Her young heart never seem to understand,
Love is a strong emotion she thinks she can handle.
Her heart accelerates in sincere purity for the one who's her lover.
No one can stop this adrenaline pouring for love desire overwhelms greatly.

Young lover, slow down. Is this, the liberty you cry about?
Your parents try to guide you on the right path but they are greeted with shout.
Estrogen triggers internal reactions as the heart hovers like a humming bird.
An inexperienced, girl will only obey. The body desires what her heart craves.

She chooses her attire as she prepares for love's altar.
Once again she slips away without her parents' consent.
They believe she is home bound in her social networking.
A parent's little angel disappears as a lady of the night without their knowledge.

She is down to earth among her peers and social circle in this game.
They go clubbing where they are engaged in activities to be relaxed.
Her heart races in sincere purity; her lover introduces an unknown substance.
She as overwhelming desires accelerating to the max by this unperceived stimulant.

An adolescent experiences trigger-happy suspense
as the world moves slowly by.
She wishes to follow the cajoling of parents but her
heart craves what her body desires.
Her body matures; the heart blossoms when experi-
ences taught her enough.
Time chastises when roles interchange, danger she
knows love drives her girl desires.

Love Raining Phases

Once my heart experienced strong wonderful momentums for you.
Crazy love was an addiction that lit the fire of desire within me anew.
Downpour mist gives an opaque cover over nature that vanishes when clouds get light.
Tis the course loves nature takes when heavy panting leads to loss of interest with fight.
When loves cohesive glue can't stick to the surface it once behold, it becomes dry.
The emotional bonds that nourished both bodies are awakened to phase of bitter cry.
Love seems to pour in phases of the rain, it appears transparent, translucent, opaque.

The blissful touch of loving bodies are engulfed with hatred so devastating like plague.
The angered misdemeanor that clothe the soul is easily read on the face
The tranquil normalcy in the home becomes beleaguered to animals trapped in a cage.
The comments we readily laughed at and overlook now create quickened fire in rage.
The favourite songs we often play to replay fade exploring new engaging portrait.
The mad feelings of blind love slowly goes away restoring the heart takes many years.
Love rains in phases, it's transparent, translucent, opaque, thunders sincerely in tears.

MAN & NATURE

This Business of Life

I often ponder the lifestyle of the birds.
They only seem to mate, sing and play.
Life seems to be just a wonderment-us game
We humans on the other hand worry a lot,
Seem like we are just characters in a plot.

Looking far ahead I saw heaps,
Out of curiosity, I investigate via close scrutiny,
Only to realize that it was the bodies of humans,
A bloody massacre caused by crime and high
tensions.

The animals never seem to worry about time
celebrations.
We on the other hand, celebrate a lot including New
Year's Day.
I often wonder if the animals join in such jolibrations.
At such times my dog is classically conditioned by a
vow to eat much.

Humans and fruits are somewhat alike my dear.
A fruit is nurtured until the plant makes it fall,
Or it is charred, bruised, cut, knocked half, knocked
down and off by man,
We fix and treat each other the same way in this
business of life.

Nature's Food Chains

Trees are rain makers in the cycle of life.
Animals and lilies add beauty to this spice,
Water flickers off the mountains from high to low.
Trees in abundance with flowers aglow,

Appearing in different shapes, colours, features
and sizes,
Everything in nature is here for a time,
All features though distinct and far,
All come together from different ecosystems.

To create a nation that is part of the universal culture,
It's a norm to neglect nature's beauty until it is gone.
Then all that is left is a faint picture in the subset,
Which interferes and upsets nature's food chains?

Society's Bangarang

You should be the first to be aware of yourself.
Trying to understand who you are will require hours of loneliness.
Self should be the most important disciple you should socialize.
This will empower you to understand the different moods that need to be colourized.

You should never be a disciple of those who walk the crooked way.
If you find yourself inflicting self wounds from day to day.
Be alert; be assertive to walk away from these bad social groups.
Investigate your looking glass self before accepting society's looking glass.

Spend each day learning the positives mores of your society.
Never forget that self should be grounded in the judiciary and legislative laws of God.
A hurricane is a cooling mechanism for summer's torrid temperature of the earth.
Society's bangarang is entrepreneurial, globalist, government against trigger-happy souls.

A child sees the world as a puzzle to learn about.
Young adults groove the daily trends of cities fashiontainment pulse beat.
The citizens of middle years are the globe's reflective practitioners.
The elders review the systems of past and present, a few engage in childhood mimicry.

Time

Mortals thesis of time is the 24 hours segmented 360° standard of measurement.
The Ancient of Day's biblical instrument began at sunset and ended at sunset.
Satan usurped God's official natural sabbatical rest of devotion and worship.
Somewhere in the timeline it was replaced and entrenched by Rome's sabbatical rest.

When the veil of time is broken every human will experience the wrath of Satan.
He will appear in white shiny bright apparel to deceive humans.
The Bible warns that a multitude and a chosen remnant will stand up for Jesus.
A glorified Satan will decree destruction for Christians in the Great Controversy.

The three angel's message warns what will happen when the veil of time closes.
God permits evil to permeate earth after the message of the eleventh hour.
God's remnants are imprisoned or hunted down in the isolated areas of earth's den.
The seven final plagues poured on sinners; God's wrath consumes and devours.

The veil of time is gradually widening to unleash demons from it vortex.
Satan smiles in acknowledgement as global evil create panic and fear.
The grandmaster of the millennium endgame rides high in major global catastrophes.

Innocent-America will put time worship to the test in the final sabbatical rest.

In eternity time is an infinite continuum with no 24 hour segmentation.
There will be no day or night for work and rest; Satan acknowledges this.
Adam and Eve had a wonderful glimpse of this endless bliss.
Satan destroyed immortal humans, angels, God in complete fellowship, I dare to miss .

Appalachian

Memories over flood of those wonderful things
we do.
You lift me high to experience the beauty of the
Appalachians.
This is where we pant at the grandeur of nature so
close in the distance.
You and I reach the stars as we romance at the
majestic Appalachians.

Memories overflow cascading and meandering as an
avalanche.
One glimpse of you reminds me of the breathtaking
view of the Appalachians.
Two silhouettes frolicking on the mountain's white
grandeur.
We're awed by nature's beauty when we sit and
ponder.

The wind whispers in the twilight of the hour.
Evergreen parades uniformly on the Appalachian's
majestic tower.
The whet ripping rhythms of the heart desires your
love on the Appalachians.
The glamorous kaleidoscope of terrianous art
displayed on nature's discourse.

Poetry Of Life

The Lord God expressed thoughts and poetry was formed.
His expression of poetry was spoken and life came into existence.
He the commander commands and creation birthed like blossom.
Life gushed, rushed and flourished from the expression of God's impression.

God's virtue touched the clay and man became a living being.
He whispered poetic sighs which opened consciousness in the soul of man.
The Lord's poetic language designs, transforms life with the will power to destroy it.
The Word orchestrated the music of poetry so unfolds the laws of nature.

Creation within all its beauty is the summary of God's poetic utterance.
Man's limited knowledge devised evolution and the big bang through ignorance.
The Word the first linguist used poetry to create the cells, atoms and the vast galaxies.
His poetry that initiated life in the beginning will annihilate sin in the second resurrection.

Jesus the Alpha and Omega is the genuine source in the poetry of life.
God the primus orator uses poetry to demonstrate he's the omnipotent force in nature.
Poetry is the freedom to express our soul not the oppressive regime of mind control.
The Word strummed each circadian rhythm of nature's life cycle bound up in poetry.

A Brief Iota

The smoke hadn't settled but you brag and boast.
About the human flame you had blown out like a burnt toast.
Mothers wail and moan about the death of their beloved one.
Are your testimonies involving human sacrifices appealing jokes?
You may feel empowered compiling a profile of human anthology.
Someday if you do not change your epitaph will read a bitter eulogy.
Every human life is a precious design unfolding into a philosophical story.

Your life is appalling, a mere speck destroying what you never created.
It's the joy of every parent to observe their precious seed develop to maturity.
A parent overture blossoming gracefully to impact both local-global societies,
Fills every heart it caresses in recollection, a seed filled with promises is removed early.
Remembrances, fondness pouring at the casket are paradigms of unfulfilled paradox.
The mind remorses with unanswered questions why a good person's life was shortened.
Fate determines with destruct the life it impinges on the crossroad to social construct.

Gerontology

I'm reflecting on what it means to grow old.
My brain sure thinks young when this body feels like it's unable to go.
A couple of years ago I walked these streets with ease quite swiftly.
Today I struggle these same streets and it feels like exercising in the snow.

Yesterday my anatomy poked many comedian acts at me.
I saw a stranger standing so I wobbled gingerly towards the scene.
The muscles pulled a sudden trick on me; I went tumbling on my knees.
I was enjoying the day in these pretty clothes when my bowels gushed like the sea.

I recall these occurred during the toddler stage hardly viewing up my world was down.
On many occasions I choked trying to swallow food and air at once.
I can't recall an exhibition technique in swallowing, trial and error was the key.
Surely it wasn't a thought; naturally I paused before releasing the bolus.

I knew nothing about speech, I screamed like a siren so everyone hurried indoor.
I crawled on all fours to gain knowledge about the earth's floor.
The concept of death meant a temporary missing in hope of returning.

I learned spiders, dogs moved, stones, sticks
remained fixed until pulled or pushed.

I was puzzled with the concepts of permanence and
constance
I didn't understand when things were hidden they
could be in the same location.
I am discovering scenes are reoccurring with this
aged childlike anatomy.
My brain rekindles to relive its toddler mimicry, this
aging, dying gerontology.

The years of manhood seems disconnected, the babe
and old seems to merge.
Now a days this old anatomy thinks it's in control
when the brain is unable to focus.
When I'm lonely and out of touch this ill tempered
will rant and scream for attention.
My anatomy has revisited it baby scene with its many
comedic funs it pokes at me.

Still

Still it lies with no apparent movement in sight.
Still this blue cover spreads with no trace of life from afar.
Still this blue-green sphere seems barren when viewed from another object in space.
Approach a little closer, every detail of life's activities is portrayed vividly within.

Still these creatures remain with eyes open-watching their bodies in static position.
Advance closer into their territory you could be consumed from its sudden attack.
Still earth's crust remains fixed for years; swift plate actions change its features in a day.
The city displays varying moods-movement-tension like Beethoven's symphonies.

In part of the city's ensemble is a mosaic of sounds in harmonious animations.
The art of pun socializations vary in settings, the drum beat of construction machines.
Appliances chip in this celebration, the horns of automobiles in traffic frustrated jams.
Machines in deep correspondence with other machines, this may be a human sacrifice,

The modern-relic three dimensional modules speak the language of designs.
Appear in contrasting colour, shape, size; width, length, volumes of characteristics.
These create the backdrop for the background music typical in every orchestra.

Still the globe rotates; day rapidly replaces night,
night with day.

Still every continent displays biomes in relation to
biomes, ecology spreads in smile.
Still the inanimate remains as the animated
relinquishes life's symphony.
Still life flourishes until disaster displaces and
annihilates many.
Still at funerals people mourn while festivals-
matrimonies increase our society.

I Could Give You A Song

What's the drama of a story without its 6 elements, ingredients?
A dancer moves majestic when her body grooves timely in a rhythms characteristic.
What is it you truly desire and miss?
This is the real stuff for your life.
I could give you a song with seductions and the vibes to hype.

When you feel this song your sighs resonate sweeter than the stuffs on iTunes.
You and I could partake in this duet in the wee hours of twilight.
Never mind those unfamiliar lines you could slow wind on each sweet chorus.
I'll make your heart cry on the bridge as you reach the peak of ecstasy.

What is the craze for a food without the four basic tastes?
In a game there must be brilliant techniques with the composure and wisdom to win.
You'll hardly ever be lonely when you sing along and wind on in rhythmic grooves.
I could appease you with the thrills of this song if you participate in this melody.

What's the vibes in this song that makes your waist gyrate in full degree?
Why does your heart race when you dance to this groove and sing along?
Our memories will be the sweetest notes to override any sad song.

The Water Cycle

'Tis the cycle of cycles, countries trade, buy and sell
goods, AI, automobile and bicycle
Its birth, childhood, adolescence, mature adult,
senescence and death for man's life cycle.
After a shower of rain falls as drizzle or downpour in
waterbodies, clay, loam and sand.
The sun beams her magnificent light rays brightly
over the ocean, sea, lake, river and land.
Her intense heat dries up liquid off land, alters water
into an invisible state through evaporation.
Then turns flowing water into water vapour in plants
leaves through the process of transpiration.
The sun's intense heat warms up skin surface, forced
sweat through its pores as perspiration.
Sweat cools the skin while it turns to an invisible
state as the sun beams on in admiration.
On sunny days the reptile species open wide their
mouths to lose water doing thermal gaping.
The dog family makes up for the lack of sweat gland
by breathing rapidly to lose water panting.
This ocean of invisible water swirls around the
environment, atmosphere as if it's escaping.

Water changing forms from one state to another, is a
real miraculous phenomenon to behold
It grooves, intermingles with dust particles high up
in the sky in temperature that's extremely cold.
In gradual momentum mist envelopes dust to forms
water droplets which begins to grow.
Gradually as the water droplets continue to expand
cotton of whiteness formed begins to flow.
As innumerable vapors grow into bigger droplets,
this cotton of whiteness expands into grey

With more droplets, this mass of grayness becomes
darken, temporarily blocking the sun's rays.
The skin receptors sense sudden coolness
descending from the atmosphere on the torrid land.
Light drizzles oftentimes descend as sensed on the
skin, especially on the surface of the hand,
Static electricity flows through the clouds as they
cluster then separate as they float on,
'Tis where it produces flashes of zigzag light that
rapidly moves across the path of the sky.
Then seconds later thunder booming baritones
resonates, it seems to enquire why,

The heavy clouds find it impossible to float over high
mountains, so it begins to unload its weight
Drizzles or downpour rapidly descends and
continues periodically to wet the land that was dry.
Downpour overflows home surround, flows from
mountains change rivers crystal look to brown.
With no path to trek on or commute along, activities
of busy people comes to halt in town.
Worrisome workers minds go homebound as rain
continues to stampede horrendously down,
'Tis a few family's realities, its money or saving earth's
natural anchorman designed to stop erosion.
Man often refuse to heed warning, makes economic
choice, won't protect trees in large portion.
Water sweeps top soil, dry grass, leaves, plastics and
varying sized objects ferociously along,
Downpour beats on roads, trees, zinc-slab roofs, fill
drums-puddles as if playing nature's song
Schools and workplaces end abruptly, this
downpour seems life threatening. Is death a joke?
Waterproof material adjust to cover over body in
varying sizes and colours, coat or cloak.

Sea of colourful semicircular devices open to shield
the user's hair and clothes from getting soaked.
Children's foot assets go into bags to hopscotch
home barefoot, or for taxi arrival some stay put.
Flood waters robust motion sometimes takes
humans in its rapid traffic by pouncing the foot.
Water races swiftly along in gutters, streams, rivers to
empty its stockpile contents at sea.
Thus hours/days later sun beams intensely, turns
liquid water into gaseous state as people plea.
The scenario changes for countries in different
climatic zones, where winter gives her icy cakes
Water vapour changes to solid below freezing point,
slowly this white solid falls as snow flakes.
It covers home grounds, landforms, yet cold
temperature crystalizes oceans, rivers and lakes.
Sun's searing heat melts ice to liquid then converts
water to its invisible state; that's what it take.

LIVING & LEARNING

Displacement Activity

What kind of man is this?
Who without the piece of stuff paper or paper stuff
Behaves like he is a boy playing with toys?
He is unable to "operate" normally in his own public.

He without the puffing stuff behaves foolishly.
He immediately becomes a man when he begins to sniff.
Decisions are clearer; problems might be solved instantly quick,
Only when he is behind his cancer stick.

He without the puffing stuff seems very nervous.
He becomes calm by taking a draw gracefully,
With lots of artistic expressions,
He releases all those internal tensions which remain unsolved.

Young boys are often fooled and confused,
About being a man only through sniffing,
'Tis reasoned males man up as giant chimney behind the cancer stick.
So, to be a man, he is psychologically pressured to his regular puffs.

Stop and think about this for a minute!
Men and Jamaica could save millions of dollars,
If they dump this rubbish and stupid form of hobby,
Your life becomes shortened just like the puffing of the stuff.

Prevail

I swore never to be soft again.
This life is a rock of hardness and coldness.
We were born in situations which makes us cry.
Yes, It's an inner cry which makes you hate life.
Rejoice in the strife, it makes you stronger in time.

I came to conquer never to fight.
I've been through tribulations which could have made me break.
With strong determination I will prevail,
Prevail, prevail, I must prevail.

Don't be afraid in the midst of a storm.
That's the time to shine bright, for beyond this blackness there's light.
We can't remain the same to discover and achieve this sight.
Just look at your inside and change your flight.

Avoid looking at the mountain just make your climb.
Don't watch the swiftness of the river as it flows by
Or you'll be unable to get on the other side.
Please believe in your beliefs, doubt your fears
Never doubt your beliefs; cause there lies an inner strength for yourself and others.

Pinch Of Shit!

What are the jewels to a snake?
Can a man predict the coming of an earthquake?
Love and materials are vanity.
A deadly woman is like a lion in disparity.

Uncomplicate complexity, it's a war against the mind,
Its like compressed air within a bottle of drinking soda.
Open the cap on the bottle and the pressure is released.
Use a similar method to eliminate worry.

Did you ever ponder on things out of reach?
It's a negative wire that can create fire.
Only money can deflate those stressful desires.
Oh Lord! Insects and pests are one big heck.

Life and going to the toilet is nearly the same.
Ups, down, anger; pain, joy, empty, filled, and rain.
All can be found when a man sweats to release a pinch of shit.
Reference or comparisons to a pinch of shit mean you are difficult to deal with.

An adult postulates a child has little things.
Children emulate adults like father God.
Adolescents articulate and formulate; tots haveunaccounted stocks.
However, an adult to a teenager is a number that is odd,
An insignificant one that cannot stop!

Life revolves around thousands of destinations.

Looking back at forty, it's eureka through deep meditation.
Recently I was a babe crying, exploring and rebelling to get attention.
Now I am leaning on a stick trying to overcome aging in hesitation.

Soraynia, Soroyia

I met these two lovely girls while teaching at primary school.
They were very attractive petals in a class dominated by bulls.
I often pondered what will be their occupations when they reach adulthood.
I'll surely be proud to see you as a teacher or doctor in your neighbourhood.

Soraynia, Soroyia be sure that you stick with your books.
Mama sent you to be educated not to be impregnated by Doctor Hook.
You can't afford to be spoilt by the devious actors who are just raging bulls.
Popularity will expire but an education is required when the teen years are full.

Dear teenagers don't be fooled by their jewellery and fancy look.
A lot of these guys only dress to disguise their ways, dem a crook.
When they achieve your middle section you'll become their publicized book.
You'll be traumatized each time your name is called in a public joke;
Here you'll be compared like a polluted brook.

Living life at this stage ones character is quickly shattered as a fallen frame of glass.
Status propagation, self esteem aren't doldrums of emotions too difficult to understand.
Self identity, the major theme tied to socialization in

society torn apart by race and class.
These daily social factors confront teens as they
emerge to become woman or man.

Long Ago

Words we speak today were used long ago
That's what I've been told.
Songs we hear today were used long ago
That's how the tunes unfold.

Crimes we have today were done long ago
The intentions were the same.
This was achieved through planning, strategizing, and deceptive ambush.
Remember yesterday's technology is no match with today's technology.

The ways we love today were created long ago
Dating, kissing, hugging; loving and romancing so and so
Bear in mind what Abraham said to Sarah "See you later my lady, you get the gist."
Always remember Herod's daughter laughed and danced the Footloose and the Twist.

Body art, tattoo designs we see today were fashionable trends that existed yesterday.
Traditions were blueprint transmitted through paintings, carvings and oral language.
This is how it goes, today's trends existed before; the cultures were multiversity.
Wait! It sounds funny, try to recall that most things were not fully documented.

Abandon

Damn what you say, sorry can't heal a broken heart.
I need no apology it can't mend how I feel inside.
I see the lies in your eyes disguised in your smile.
Which is hardest to bear? Is it your hurt, the repetition
of your apology, or lies?

Don't you know love disintegrates when you take this
union for granted?
How can you cry when there is no demonstration of
love from the inside?
Girl! Don't you know when love hurts you'll be left
abandoned.
Your repetitive apology from the hurt can't
compromise the state of being abandoned.

No longer am I your intimate Allegro Con Brio that
vividly expresses your day.
This body is engulfed with bitterness that makes it
quakes from your jealous plays.
Yet this body aches to touch the hard and icy persona
of you.
It's the state of desiring someone, but crushed by the
fate of being abandoned.

Those sleepless nights I prayed for this stressful
devastation to go away.
The sweet sensations of those memories are deeply
embedded in this morbid pain.
Love accelerating gracefully above becomes
wormwood when it ends at the fall.
I stood tall at the edge of the cliff, suspended in the
grandeur merged with danger.

Words

I lay in bed as the Abba tunes played.
My train of thought came at a pause by the ringing of the phone.
Your speech was so compact, fiery on contact; it disturbed my emotional state of mind.
Words had erased in a few seconds what we had fabricated for years.

I was in a state of shock; your words had exploded like a bomb.
I felt like a scolded child with pent up words but my tongue went numb.
Can we review this situation before you bow out in grace?
My world sucked into a black hole with the worded bomb "it's over'.

I underestimated the value you offered that molded this man.
I became unthankful for the fulfillment and stability you brought to my life.
I replaced my precious diamond for tainted gold.
My world was over like a rudderless ship sailing purposely in the sea of humanity.

Words break, words recreate, words modify the state of the heart.
Words shape, words touch, words personify the person I am.
Words reassure, words care, words demonstrate the way we were socialized.
Words wound, words abuse, words warn, communicating the way I feel.

Two-Faced Persona

This is the lachrymose self-expression we must face.
You can't hide behind your friends forever.
Your body language reveals the story of sorrow.
The smiles disguised as pain reads you are a Jezebel anyway.

You can pretend today when you take someone for granted.
The story of your body language reveals the Jezebel in you.
It is hard to accept this persona that intimately overwhelms within.
Heaven knows I couldn't take your dramatic blues anymore.

Girl sometimes glimpses of your heart reveal.
These deceptive contents sown in your moods lying underneath,
You maybe were smiling while your heart cries.
The mirror of reality haunts silently when you take a friend for granted.

Your body blasts from the moods it avalanches.
How long can you bear this two-faced persona you wear?
You may think you are hiding behind your friends; they know it's your defense.
In the years to come the mirror of reality finds you guilty with no pretense.

The Human Commodity

When you think you are in love with a friend who is not that special one.
You did not perceive this relationship was built on sinking sand.
For years she pretended to be although you cohabitate with her.
She only rode the years with you; you did not understand this was her intention.

My friend you can imagine the heartbreaks you'll face.
The tearful cries of heartaches and pain wandering many days,
Then you'll know it's time to let go the Giddy House you embrace.
You never waste your precious days dreaming about hopelessness.

When you think you are this special one.
You fabricate your life around a friend you've known for years.
The promises disappear, you will never wear the wedding ring.
Your families and friends rejoice you know this deceptive pretense.

When you believe you can trust your companion.
Who substitutes your character to be with the popular name brand?
These, the material craze, where humans are treated as disposable friends.
Humans like commodity for now the trend exist to be replaced by another one.

Dream Big

Big dream or dream big and you will achieve.
Remember great wonders are achieved by the miniature ants.
They struggle with giant loads to store for the winter.
The state of destitution is the search for answers that remain unsolved for now.

The failure to initiate is the greatest defeat one receives with pain.
Each of us faces our hour of destitution like glimpses of a picture.
Remember the state of perfection comes with hours of lonely practices and rejection.
The hour of recognition and inauguration is the home-run one receives for long practice.

Those who accept honour without the baptism of fire will be exposed with failure.
Remember no animal achieves mastery of its body physiology without hours of practice.
The Creator designated time to be nature's sculpture for every image that was formed.
The greatest destitution of spirit involves having all the money, materials but no "food".

Peace returns after a natural disaster and deep reflection after a great catastrophe.
Famine of the mind esteems spiritualism, sorcery, occult symbols anathema to Jesus.
Human catastrophes unfold with three meaning: philosophical, spiritual and physical.
Space probing, evolution and spiritualism are neo-faiths replacement for the Bible.

When Things Go Wrong

When things go wrong find a solution to the tsunami that overwhelms.
When things go wrong remember the unseen foe may have petitioned God to sift you.
When individuals strategize to create discord to upset your circadian rhythms,
Remember the brain reasons, the spinal cord reacts; think about consequences.

Our attitudes should be like Biblical instruments deciphering Satan's daily tsunami.
When things go wrong don't anticipate with anger and hallucinate.
When things go wrong temporarily walk away to a tranquil environment,
A peaceful place is healthy for mental focus, critical analysis and reloading.

Both good and bad conditions unfold like a thought with new perspective.
The highlight of a character is revealed with precision in the midst of a crisis.
A thing going wrong is like atmospheric brown clouds invading our comfort zone.
The same way survivors fight to get oxygen; you should be alert to withstand the crisis.

Crisis in life is like a mist or fog hovering for a while until it disappears.
Each condition comes at an opportune time, or while facing or plunging into a pitfall.
Some crises you'll be prepared to meet headlong; others appear sudden and unaware.

When things go wrong be calm, say a prayer and
read a psalm
Necessities for the ball.

Love's Documentary

Picture love documentary taken with a foreground and a background!
He was at the focal point always in the foreground.
I was always there in the background but hardly could be seen.
When you were with your friends, he was the main character in the scene.

Each of us as met a lover who hardly gave us recognition.
You place your all, believing you achieve but the main character is out of reach.
As the play unfolds towards the end you realize you'll be the incognizant one.
It's always bitter when you recognize you're never treated with equality.

As the years go by you meet strange people who paint in the tainted spot.
Then a few characters come along who place you in the forefront.
How do you handle a friend who submits only to be in the star role?
They may not fight but their life choice is to be painted in the foreground.

Every human is a pragmatic painter who places people in these two scenes.
We have our choice to walk away when you know they'll place you in the background.
It can't be right to live your life in the shadow of those who decide to treat you unfairly.
A lover specializes with one on the intimate level and the other on the superficial tier.

Work Is Slavery

Being taught and prepared for an adult world,
Through confession it's very hard and confusing,
As a kid who is about to emerge from school,
Career talks and taking subjects, these are my necessary tools.

Work is slavery leaving home too early in too much despair.
Work is slavery labouring for hours and getting little or nothing.
Work is slavery my qualifications are in malice with my pay.
Work is slavery this Babylon system a kill all nation and innocent man.

I can hardly afford to spend those moments at home
With my spouse and lovely kids who daily I'm separated from.
Constantly rushing to and fro to labour for Babylon.
What use is getting and not showing love to my spouse and kids?

Coming home and going to work with this mental trap.
Wondering where will the next meal and things will appear.
Working hard and hardly eating can lead to malnutrition.
Still having no chain but as a slave rebelling against this one.

I'm a Man Who Cares

Early yesterday I said something which made you
hurt.
This often happens when we curse.
Please don't fight try, and understand.
Oh! Babe why grow angry for my silence.

Lady I'm a man who cares.
It's very hard to express what's inside.
I tried and tried but still I can't express this love that
lies deep within.
Can't you see that my personality is constructed deep
within?

I just want to hold you and caress you tenderly.
Give you all the feelings which lie deep inside.
Daily you nag me about trivial matters.
The tripping of your tongue only leads to disparity.

These lonesome feelings are eating my inside.
Don't you know I need you here?
Please make this my special day.
We do our best romantic play.

Silence

The multidimensional use of the word silence varies in significance.
Traveling in one direction, silence engages in an endless expanse of space.
Silence loco motes on animals of prey that suffers vehement attacks from predators.
One victim posits "silence is fear with constant pain of knowing or exposing".

This multipurpose instrument connotes tranquility of mind and soul.
The negative mechanism reads laughter on the outside to disguise painful abuse.
Silence the command wrecks customers through services in bureaucratic systems.
The quietude of this disease havocs an internal system in gradual decay.

This deadly weapon moves swiftly like stealth carrying out an ambush.
In reverse it operates surgical attacks within a specific location on its target.
It is the colourful camouflage of animals within it's or an environment.
Silence uses the device of mind control via religious-political one world government.

Silence engulfs opportunities through monopoly of nature's documentary.
It traps like quicksand consuming gradually as the victim's protest.
This defying process operates like a black hole to hold the galaxies with its gravity.

Silence is nature's noiseless; serenity can be
transformed like an earthquake.

The elites orchestrate the bosses, every oath instruct
the others to obey the command.
This process involves persuasions or compulsory
coercions to worship Babylon.
It whispers scandalous exposures or demolitions to all
disciples who snub instruction.
The contract killer delivers the final sentence; the
body sags like its in prayer.

Moulded in the solitary habitat of the womb, Jacob
and Esau had many conflicts.
It's the total institution where isolated humans
remorse for their guilt.
The sacred place to develop inner virtues, meditate
and leisurely read in peace.
Dreams and inventions are conceptualized in the
lonely hours where it's serene.

Life's Sentence

This is the pain I inferred dealing with a superficial
friend.
A second chance is an error which torments me to
the very end.
A woman's deceptive attitude is quite as deadly as
global warming mechanisms.
Gradually a man's image and reputation disintegrate
when he's treated as nothing.

A genuine man experiences pain to cushion his
woman.
The traffic creates pain whenever I'm in haste.
With the sun bursting in anger, the mind decries
conditions of red, green congestions.
Ice melts with global warming mechanisms; car's
greenhouse effects make me sweat.

A fiancée or wife becomes the topic sentence in a
man's life story.
She's the predicate that warrants sentence agreement
with the subject.
As an apostrophe she possesses or shows ownership
of her mate.
A man will be incomplete with those burst of
excitement and disapproving yuck.

Man's disorganized activities need order, regrouping;
she's colon in her operation.
A woman punctuates every sentence of a man's life
with her distinguish marks.
When love ends in a circle the lady appropriates a
man's surname by becoming his Mrs.
Her unworthiness is like the comma splice
fragmenting life's sentence with shame.

Frozen Cold

From something radiating beauty unfolds foliage of cruel conditions.
Somehow my accurate perception proved you were a mass of deception.
I was enjoying the snow unaware it was growing ugly cold.
My body shook like a terrible tremor until I experienced blizzards.

I thought everything would be good the day your rays shone on me.
I could never fathom your mirage that glittered beyond the road.
It was like experiencing the sun when all around was frozen cold.
My body shivered on ice, where were you to keep me warm.

I was the lonely man wandering along this sea of ice.
It felt like traveling mars, the barren planet with only bitter cries.
All around,I experienced hopelessness amid this sheet of ice pulling me to the ground.
Nature so tranquil tried to sacrifice me with it eerie scenes and ghostly sound.

I've experienced Antarctica's icy persona on her glamorous white.
Her love was the drama that brought frostbite conditions in my life.
In this frigid arena lacking love, will the sun's heat be able to melt the snow?
I saw her rays beyond the horizon when all around

was frozen cold.
When the twilight arose everywhere, the white appeared like ghosts.
I heard the creatures howl in the dark but I feared death the most.
You my ray of hope wasn't there when all around was frozen cold.
It was this experience of not seeing the sun when all around me was icy ground.

It's been couple of days in the snow and hope won't be soon.
I've been exhausted traveling all along when my body felt numb.
In this frigid arena without the sun, my world seems down.
Her ray was an illusion beyond the horizon yet I was trapped and frozen cold.

Beware!

Today the world seems strange
There was no you anymore.
The rain poured heavily but I walked through it caring no more.
All the confusing scenes of love had erupted openly and buried beneath.
Daily before she reacted like grains of sand operating in my shoe.

Today I'm standing alone reviewing the worth of your grace.
Sincerity blossoming from the heart surely is expressed on the face.
The rain poured heavily but my heart was expressing this condition.
Internal tensions reacting to love's drama caused sweat to profuse through the skin.

When the clouds are filled with water, they release rain to become lighter.
Unanswered burdens are deep well emotions that makes a lady cry.
Men operate like machines ignoring faults until facing mechanical failure.
Relationships lacking purpose and direction are emotional sores to let go for sure.

Today I had to face her, but I was scared with fear.
The concept of safety had totally disappeared with the water missile underneath.
A few bridges collapsed under the gale force of troubled waters.
Beware! Pauses and limitations are efficient warnings

Politics & Religion

Mount Vaticanus

They say the number 7 stands for perfection,
But could it also stand for deception?
Sette colli di Roma (Seven hills of Rome) is Vaticanus the whore of revelation.
Ask that whoring gal that sits on its Vat to con us.

Religious groups and countries pay homage to this Transnational State.
This humble lion is a gruesome dragon
Which has entered the millennium endgame the primus dictator innocent as a lamb?
Ask that whoring gal that sits on its Vat to con us.

Her laws are omnipotent and can decide your fate.
The ominous construction for the soul is the insurmountable Devil's gate.
Which sends you to heaven or hell with lugubrious excommunication?
Ask that whoring gal that sits on its Vat to con us.

Her documents are immutable and enter the nation's parliament as stealth.
The world was mesmerized, awe-stonished by the Christmas fiesta of the Beloved 11.
Cinderella broke the world with her Gramscian shoe.
These chameleon portraits, conceives the Immaculate Heart, sits on her Vat to con us.

The world and Thumbelina's situation room is unholy.
The chamber of imagery the prophet Ezekiel decried and murmured.
The hideous creature with tiara written 666 disguised in Latin using Roman numeral.

Ask that whoring sin thing that sits on its
Vat to con us.

The pope's authority is likened to God with the
beatification and canonization of saints.
Do priests vow to practice celibacy or to celebrate
the batty?
The church indoctrinates men to fornicate daily at its
wormwood fountain.
Ask that whoring gal that sits on its Vat to con us.

Global Ecumenism

The propagation of groups from tribes to nations,
To regional syndicates enmeshed in the borderless world,
It signifies the unholy trinity: Dies Dominica, the microchip, and the biometric system.
The geopolitical system of finis grandeur; the cadere to global economic collapse!
The dividendum of earth: the wise Jacob,
The prayerful Daniel, the "licky", "licky" Esau, and the heinous Cain.

Lucifer's comfortare to worship the divus image Dies Dominica;
Immortalized A.D. 324 to usurp the biblical Sabbath memor:
The omega command or executare for Christus true remnants;
The global amalgamation of religious-political agenda:
Through persecution, recrimination, and discrimination.

The Lone Wolf was once a mighty religious-political hegemony.
Her power was broken by the Little Red Riding Hood's French brother.
Her status was restored, and she is now riding high.
Waiting on a specific Marian apparition to miraculously happen in the sky.

Lucifer was never, can never, and will never be omnipotent.
He isn't omnipresent, doesn't know the daily

activities, thoughts of every human.
The use of satellite tracking devices with powerful resolution
Can identify every human through the microchip.
'Tis part of Lucifer's Vatican plan to monitor, dictate the globe through a new world order.

Caesar Augustus' global ecumenism has been refashioned in a postmodern world.
The biometric system, the microchip, and the TRN are like personal identity number.
This provides vital information about every sphere of one's life by the touch of a button.
Dissolution of national borders is replaced like it or not
By the welcoming of a new world order.

Life's Three Degrees

The initiation towards achieving a first degree is a child's paradox.
It can be compared with a baby who begins
To explore its home community to gain experience.
The reading for bachelor's degree is like a shift in one's mental paradigm
To attain tertiary tier infrastructure through trial and error. it is the growth, maturation,
Development of human resources to be fitted in a credential society.
The physical attainment of a first degree may be compared to a spiritual walk.

We are expected to apply similar principles through studying,
Research, hard work in attaining enlightenment and success.
Man is expected to seek and search for life's purpose
And meaning to fulfill his destiny
It involves finding answers through education about good and evil.
At the master level of studying surface research becomes shattered.
The tutor expects the pupil to go indepth in order

To gain deeper meaning and understanding.
Facts must be deduced and proven, and parts fabricated inductively in blocks logically.
Spiritually the Lord expects his children to master an understanding of His character.
We are to discern the physical crisis around, identifying the invisible force as its initiator.
Our physical conditions and orientations are being

sculpted by life's turmoil and bliss.
A dissertation at the doctorate level involves processing
A sample thoroughly using an archeologist approach.
Here in-depth applications, technical skills, mental competency,
And discipline in a special field of study should include participatory observation.
In a spiritual context the LORD desires us to fit
The various glimpses of His nature from the Bible,
The natural world and the invisible spirit world. Hence,
We are to diligently study each glimpse of

His character portrait then applies it to our own flawed nature.
The internet contains infinite data that are legitimate and illegitimate.
Here an archeologist approach is a necessary precaution.
Similarly, there are countless biblical data to be learnt and
Applied through an intricate study of Jesus' infallible or flawless character.
Inversely, there are innumerable debauchery to be avoided
This prevents snaring and contamination in Satan's infirmary.

Global Discombobulation

It is man, ethnic groups, races; nations, and the globe
progressing to auto-destruction.
This process is offset by the make-believe attitude
developed in virtual reality.
Virtual reality is portrayed as normal socialization.
War, terrorism, religious indoctrination; suicide
bombers, kidnapping:
Everywhere becomes a hotspot for civil unrest, militia
ambush;
And a fire brigade response through world policing,
Our civil liberties are overtaken, and are replaced by
panic, insecurity, and global fear.

The chameleon traps of Home Land Security,
surveillance society, the metal detector;
The microchip, wiretapping, electronic tagging, alarm
systems and FEMA.
Gosh! Humanity is on the very bloody path of a
virtual new world order.
Man finds comfort in the physical and electronic
protections that are rather useless.
Who guards us from the attack of demons and human
spirits
Which easily overrides and go undetected through
our toy and plastic security systems?

The social ills of human trafficking, environmental
rape, degradation, unemployment;
Drug smuggling, patent and electronic piracy are
consequences which go unsolved.
These avalanches into family decay, moral decay,
Community garroting; national trauma, and
international recession

God's angels are withdrawing: John the Revelator prognosticates through warnings.
It's Daniel's time of trouble, we the characters partake in this Great Controversy.
Decency is replaced by indecency, sanity is overtaken by insanity, good seems evil;
Evil appears good, as the modernity disappears rapidly for the post-modernity.

Hey! Look! It is the international culture shop parade:
Mac Donaldization, Disneyization, Ford, General Motors, Toyota, Motorola; Reebok, Tommy Hilfiger, Nike, and
Cooyah for prestige, self-assurance, and to boost one's ego.
It is the biting of Apple into our civilization
With its gadgets for our personal convenience: Mac book, iPod, iPad; iPhone,
There's the Microsoft Xbox, Sony's play station, and the endless gaming.

In addition, there are the neo-worship phenomenon: the New Age crystals, therapy,
Self help books; transcendental meditation, increase in euthanasia, spiritualism;
Indulgence (salvation sold to pardon and pay for sins), Marian apparitions,
The Catholic Massacre; memorials for the dead, Krishna fellowship,
Psychoanalysis, superheroes, Hollywood, Nollyhood and Bollyhood,
Man becomes god, vying strongly to replace Jesus and the Lord God Almighty.
Satan the mendacious spirit hollers! He is aware of the eleventh hour.

His campaign becomes bolder in a desensitized and
Directionless globe insensitive to the Bible's power.

Money ripens convenience. Our conveniences are
credited or paid for by money.
This process involves hyping, tourist trekking,
partying,
Massage palour(ing), prostituting, sporting,
electronic and cyber telecommuting, palm and
psychic readings,
DVD watching, plus the countless ways of
entertaining.
The rapid socialization process, in this quick fix society
continues
To propagate through the compression of time as an
important meal of lynchpin.
One transnational corporation's elation becomes a
global frustration.
Is this all part of the global security or insecurity?
Surely this is the combination of confusion and
diffusion of ideologies and
Hi-tech gadgets as man operates as a robotic remote
of condifussion.

Hero in Your Life

There are times in our lives, when human actions hurt like knives.
And there's no help to guide you to the light.
Just call silently to God in prayer and you'll be surprised.
Jesus is the propitiator in your life; he'll free you from these emotional tides.

There are times in our life when you cry.
Because the reality of life has burden inside,
Just search for the Word our Advocate who lives inside.
And he'll rescue you from the emotional sighs.

He senses when you cry.
That's where he stays all the time.
He knows you're hurting inside.
Our savior is the real hero in your life!

In The Flash Of A Moment

In the flash of a moment there's a lot of praise.
In the flash of a moment this could be your distaste.
In the flash of a moment our laughter turns to sorrow.
Our days are numbered for life to appear and go.

In the flash of a moment times flies away,
In the flash of a moment a life is made.
In the flash of a moment the young become old.
Life becomes more complicated the older one grows.

Everyday it's the same with the future it's uncertain,
No one but Jesus knows for sure where life is going.
Scientists are searching, soothsayers are
prognosticating.
But in the moment of a flash our forms will change.

Cheirographon

LORD! This heart is torn apart.
I'm caught in crossfire.
I am longing to serve you, this is my true desire.
Whenever I'm in tuned to do thy will, my world becomes shattered.
My heart wants to be in deep communion with you Jesus.
This mind is in a constant fight to overcome wrong for right.
There are hours I am left destitute.
And your presence seems far out of reach.

Cheirographon! For the years I lived for myself.
Cheirographon! When I refused to intercede on behalf of others;
Cheirographon! For refusing to believe you closed the doors of my past.
Cheirographon! Oh LORD! For the powers you gave but I refused to use.
Cheirographon! For the knowledge I withheld to nurture the seed in another.
Cheirographon! The light becomes a stumbling block for others.
Cheirographon! I cursed instead of becoming a blessing to my fellow man.
Cheirographon! For the moments I gossip, backbite, and backstab my neighbours.

Reminiscing the years I should have been your soldier.
Marching fiercely to proclaim mercy and forgiveness at the cross;
There were moments I tried desperately to believe.

The days I gave up eagerly walking back on those fallow grounds.
The many hours I spent arguing relentlessly seeking answers to life greatest phenomenon.
I momentarily gave up the faith desperately and walked away.
I searched wholehearted with my soul and spirit but you seemed locked away.

Thank you Jesus for the court role you play as the middle man.
Pleading my case before your Father in whose sight sin cannot stand.
Jesus all my imperfections you take so I may be pure before the Almighty One.
Lord Jesus you are both the heavenly High Priest and the sacrificial Lamb.
All the righteous sins oh Lord you place on the head of the he-goat Satan.
This redemptive process makes us blameless before the Day of Atonement.
Thy judgment is twofold: protecting the blameless and destroying the blemish.

The Delay

There seems to be a painful lingering heartache when one experiences a delay.
I am in hesitation to get my assignment on time but my computer broke down.
I walked away in anger and frustration because of this insignificant setback.
I yearned for the day for the date or excursion to come.
My fiancée fabricated the greatest excuse which magnified the hatred of this scum.

I'm frenzied and in pain to release this toxic bomb.
I'm several metres away from home to read and relax on my throne.
It's my rush hour as I give Asafa Bolt to the door of this important throne.
Gosh! I am in pain and shock at my greatest discomfiture.
A relative of mine sits and moan on the family's comfort zone.
I am sweating, pacing the floor doing the Jim Screechy, Bogle and the Gully Creeper.
Trying desperately to hold this uncomfortable load you know!

The public transport is an unusual medium to be in.
There you are bombarded with a panorama of different genre of music.
It is the mobile market place to whisper to an associate, to greet a would be lover,
To vent ones pent up feelings; to argue celebrity's lifestyle,
Debate social issues including the family,

The community, politics; religious and pastoral saga.
The conductor utters "fare please!"
it's impossible to reach my pocket when the bus is packed like a slave ship.
This is a nasty setback.
My uneasiness causes the "ducta" to react like
The comedians Oliver Samuels, Brother Desmond and Maama man.

My brain is on fire as it warns of a double dilemma.
My left leg is paralyzed with a tingling feeling
Moving rapidly like the beaming of an emergency light.
I bellow "ah!" as my body shivers to its total capacity of water which makes me cramp.
I'm puzzled wondering which of these pains is the hardest to bear.
The bus comes to a halt at Half Way Tree, but I am two stone's throw away from the park.
I am unable to loco mote swiftly because one leg feels normal while the other is numb.
This surely is a bitter delay, the traffic moves freely on green but my bladder signals red.
Finally I arrived at the destination, in queue I waited my turn, dis weighty wait dread
Urgently I unleash this tension, I wet my underwear, in my pants this dampness spread.

Time becomes weighty burdens as delays add to tons of disappointments.
The customers rant and scream at workers in the bank.
Patience is replaced by infuriated trigger-happy emotions.

Humans curse another human instead of understanding the bureaucratic system.
Inconvenience is a gruesome delay on ones precious time.
You dial the cell phone to express an important concept or thought.
The speaker blurs in your ear "you have reached the voice mail box of #".
This makes you yell "what the Felony Under Carnal Knowledge is this!"

At the maternal ward the families grapple with this fearful happy suspense.
Tis the grievous shriek of this disgusting setback.
A woman wails and moans from the pain to release her little bundle of joy.
Her amniotic sac ruptures but her doc told her it was not yet her hour.
She shivers and sweats like she just had her shower.
In labour a woman's greatest fear the bisect power known as the Caesarean procedure.
It's the Freddy Krueger thriller that haunts the room like the silent killer.
We say the Lord's Prayer for the safe delivery of the baby and protection of its mother.

Our humanness suggests that a delay is a setback,
Or retrogression, or hindrance from progressing forward.
The master of pain and disillusion, the great Satan hinders or
Delays our quest for finding the truth about the Lord God Almighty.
He set up blockage through human agents, natural/ man-made catastrophes, and crisis.

This prevents one from gaining insights about the Lord God Almighty.
Tis the memory of painful failures, chides the mind warning of impending danger.
Delay in the biblical sense is rather an important event about a merciful and loving God.
He delays the impending judgment that all may come to repentance.
(2 Peter chapter 3)

The Power of Jesus Resurrection

Are you amazed we humans have become the insignificant other?
We were brushed aside from our paradise by deception and disobedience.
Satan's apparition hypnotized our parents
To the transgressed he gained victory over humanity.
The Lord God Almighty could not bear to be in our presence,
Sin had created this chasm.
Heaven had to compromise its highest celestial being to pay the wages of sins.

Jesus died as our sacrifice in order to buy us back to God.
The celestial hosts all mourned the suffering and death of their beloved savior.
Today Laodicean's have rejected the creation and resurrection in place of evolution.
Sin's effect caused humans to become mortal and to experience physical death.
Yeshua's death and resurrection power had spared
The human race the fate of eternal death and separation.
He had to become one of us in order to gain experience.

The effect of eternal death and separation
Jesus bore, wailed and mourned a painful death
To be prefigured in order to achieve preeminence.
How can I fathom the mystery and majesty of the cross?
It genuinely provided the litmus test and the only provision for humanity's salvation.

Lucifer's initiation gained hegemonic status over
God's authority on earth at the fall.
Jesus' birth, death and resurrection conquered Satan
once and for all.

Satan cannot deny the pragmatic phenomenon of
Jesus' death and resurrection.
He can only sideline and highlight the laws of karma,
the reincarnation of the body,
And the immortality of the soul to weaken its appeal.
In addition, he has tarnished the gold creation with
the dross evolution.
The object lesson of the cross and the resurrection
cannot
And will not be damned by Satan or any millions of
year bone discovery ramification.
In the first resurrection the saints will rise immortal
beings to be with Jesus.

They will reign one thousand years in heaven
Where queries will be made about absent friends and
loved ones.
Answers will be provided when they view the books
of records of each human deed.
Eternal death and separation for every sinner
Whose names are not written in the book of life;
Here they will be totally annihilated with Satan and
His demons in the lake of fire in the second
resurrection.

Genuflection

Will you pledge allegiance to the savior Jesus or to the number 666?
The Bible records this number on three occasions.
Cyrus declared liberty for thousands of Israelites including 666 children of Adonikam.
They returned from captivity in physical Babylon to physical Jerusalem. (Ezra 2:13)
The Revelator John predicts the establishment of Satan's kingdom by the leader with the 666 symbol in spiritual Babylon
He will use Esau's compliance to prevent millions
From reaching (Revelation 13-20) the heavenly New Jerusalem
The world is at its definitive crossroad of sanctions and
Embargoes in one systematic control over our souls.

The economist Solomon used his wisdom to collect 666 weight of gold in annual trade. (2 Chronicles 9:13)
The primus antichrist in Vatican Rome will introduce
The one world government to replace global commerce at earth's greatest catastrophe.
Here each human must decide whether to reject or accept Satan's mark,
This coercion will help to determine the camp an individual is in after the eleventh hour.
Will you genuflect to the savior Jesus or the destroyer Satan?
Worship and food influenced man to transgress at the fall.
It will once again be the authentic spiritual test before Christ's Second Advent.

The LORD wants his children to know that in
The midst of their deepest oppression he is still they're only hope.
Stand in faith he cajoles, rejecting Satan's mark will be the greatest test you will face.
Your master Jesus will come down at that significant hour of doubt
And death threats to liberate you from Babylon's tyranny.
This testimony can be attested to the movement of the spirit of
The Lord on Cyrus to unshackle his children from Babylonian cruelty.

The Apostle Paul

Who was this man that killed many in the early church?
He carried letters of agreement to kill Christian who opposed the Sanhedrin Council.
He the eyewitness to Stephen's death massacred Christians in a major blood bath.
This noted orator was born in Tarsus; a Jewish law student whom Gameliel taught.

Many claim that Peter, the other apostles and Jewish Christians
Practiced and taught only the Jewish traditions.
Gosh! What a lie!
They even claimed he who consented to Stephen's death initiated the Jesus movement.
Hey! Satan's agents are sly.

The critics say "he was never one of the original twelve,
Had never seen Jesus but only learned his teaching after the Messiah's death".
Human limitations and insufficient knowledge should question;
Avoid distorted and fallacious judgments about the Bible and its Author.

Saul who became Paul had an encounter with the immortalized Jesus.
Remember he was traveling with his company to kill early Christians in Damascus.
He was hit by the Savior's mysterious lightning; where he got blinded,
Fell off his horse where Jesus outlined his future

Christian career.
He fasted three days, was cajoled, appointed, restored; and anointed by Ananias
Who instructed him about the path it takes to become Jesus' warrior.

Look! This is not funny. Paul started preaching to the Jews but was denounced.
This hot contention caused a split in the congregation.
Some believed he was changed, others scoffed he's a chameleon who killed Christians.
His life was speared by genuine Christians who let him over a wall in a basket.

A Pharisee denied by his Jewish brethren turned his focus to the gentile world.
The fearless persecutor becomes the fiery bold preacher.
Salvations truth he taught to people who he says were God's creature.
He was acknowledged by Peter to be Christ's minister to both the Jew and gentile fold.

Termites

Termites build their nests under the altar.
The Devil knows you are a disaster Christian with the Laodicean chameleon character.
Hey! Christian with the flawed character, don't point finger at the heathen and backslider.
God knows that rottenness is destroying you to nothingness; he wants you to be a star.

Demons and termites work in life are somewhat similar.
They invade your home undetected at any hour.
Both enter houses through avenues that are unprotected.
Once the habitat becomes comfortable the process of decay will end in annihilation.

Termites build dirt roads in God's structure.
They move unaware like stealth until the building is devoured.
Once the structure is infested it's a life long war to defeat, control these creatures.
It involves frustration at reentrance, stressful encounters, panic introducing measures.

God's warning every Christian to be alert of these invisible warriors.
Their subtle attacks go unnoticed until it permeates the entire structure.
Their initiation, infestation develops into life long struggle in overcoming these creatures.
This spiritual ramification unfolds, physical manifestation with philosophical connotation.

Termites are gradually eating away the church structure.
They are adjusting and reproducing a new colony after the poison.
These offspring are bred to resist and overcome the toxic substance.
Dear Christians only the Holy Spirit guards, make us aware of this invisible destruction.

The Post Modern Generation

Onlookers are awestruck by the multiversity
of dimensions displayed by the post modern
generation.
Their egos are wide and bold to the face like urban
sprawl.
Culture and identities are malleable and tied to
fashionable name brands.
They are fragile and appear invisible when they are
not wearing one.

These children are born with a blueprint to harness
modern technology.
Adults at certain age take several days to decipher
the general use of a gadgets button.
Post modern children maneuver gadgets within hours
making complexities appear simple.
They seem to master the gadgets fixtures by a quick
understanding of its features.

Their faces appear to be a rework of the modern art.
Many consult the unusual bleaching lotion or the
official plastic surgeon.
It's not a rare occasion to see a Negro with two
distinct complexions.
The post modern generation doesn't appreciate the
two dimensional Edwardian art.
They are the three dimensional module of the neo-
modern twist of this Renaissance.

See it's the damning nature of your material love I
perceive.
Do you value the characters of human or the
incentives of mere paper worth?

Here humans are treated as commodities to be used and refused as disposables.
Tis the philosophy, pragmatism, social orientation of the children of the post-modernity.

The Hardness of the Law

How long can your terror reign on this land?
At the age of eighteen you removed your old man.
You're twenty years with the wisdom of an old jackal,
The look in your eyes portrays the lifeless landscape
of a barren wilderness.

You are always on the run; the society will hunt you
down.
You are trapped in this murderous continuum like a
fox on the hunt.
You are a menace who will one day face the hardness
of the law.
They know that no one could match you the trigger-
happy king.

The people traded in town but at the mentioned of
your name the shutters came down
A hardened man reacts softly when he faces the
hardness of the law.
He's a broken spring without positive tension that
creates illicit harmony in society
The untouchable fragile run will end face to face with
the hardness of the law.

Satan cannot save you when the Lord hits you with
the hardness of his just laws.
The Eternal Outlaw insurrection will end with the
institution of God's governance.
Here he'll face the hardness of God's law on that
special Day of Judgment.
My friends, the hardness of earth's laws will
be a testament of God's covenant with man.

Amid Patience ...Wait

Amid every bad situation Lord, you are our hope and bliss.
Waiting for good tidings may be positive like the oceans up thrust.
It's the enthusiastic elation for your nail-biting patience.
The heart races, the brain pours praises for the stagnating pause of that reward.

Amid every catastrophic condition Lord, patience may be the gift.
Good tidings may be the tag prize for a purpose that may be elusive.
The body releases adrenaline in expectation for the prize of that special occasion.
Deep undercurrent forces body collapse, without the prize comes disappointment.

Amid the ton weight of mishaps Lord, comprehending patience is a pause.
Evil appears boldface with short lived dominance amid prestige, fame-alluring beauty.
Good seems recessive, the dull dragging feelings that drains one enthusiastic energy.
In the end evil accelerates into a pitfall, good elevates from the ashes for infinity.

Amid our patience for good tidings Lord, we pause for a reasoned cause.
Waiting is a weight suspended on the cord of invisible time in future.
Patience weighs heavily on time's balance amid expected elation or sudden death.

The Lord's coming is suspended on time's invisible
cord to be free at God's command.

Amid the weight suspended on the time of wait,
patience becomes suspense.
The reward is the cliffhanger, creates thrills-fright
overrides-overburdens patience.
The home run fulfilled, many will genuflect before
Jesus as countless face death.
Amid patience, God's prize suspends in suspense; we
should endure this weight. Wait!

Backsliding Heart

I have been marching down sin's road.
Satan's maze hid the cross; I can't pretend I'm lost there's no insight.
With no hope on the horizon I'm battered by the enemies of the dark.
I am fighting to hold my head above the waves of sin,
I will not sink.

Where did I lose my footing on Jesus the rock?
Lord forgive my backsliding heart.
When I lose spiritual focus in this world caving in,
How much further in life should I sink in sin?

Satan's grip is too strong; many times I err, although I acknowledge Jesus my savior.
How much further in life will I bring shame to your name?
Help this backsliding heart to renew its way to salvation's home.
How did I regress this far from you Lord?

I never imagined toying with sin would have slowly broken me.
I'm a plant whose root is not anchored on Jesus the rock.
I disobeyed the prayerful pleas of the saints and slowly transgressed the way.
How much further in sin should I be dragged by the arch-enemy of the cross?

Blood

Blood the universal jargon springs from a religious symbolic tree.
Scientists theorize blood ships nutrients, oxygen, hormones and metabolic wastes.
The economist, entrepreneur knows it implies trade: goods, services, human relations.
Bloodletting, bloody contentions originated with Cain and ends at the Second Advent.

For Jews blood signifies the sacrifice of oxen, he goat, and lamb.
The blood of these animals was taken to the high priest.
He stood before God the Father asking for pardon for you and me.
The lamb, its blood pointed to Jesus the Lamb; heavens High Priest atoning our sins.

The drinking of blood atones occult worshippers to the Father of lies.
It is a contract and sale leading to bondage, corruption and death.
The occult disciples sell their soul cutting their flesh, signing names in bloody contracts.
Christians know Jesus died once for all, sinful self dies gradually, the Holy Spirit contact

Blood, the symbolic covenant leads to death thus gaining eternity into heaven.
It is the sacred tenet where Christians and sinners repent and plea at God's mercy seat.
Doctrines about the afterlife with no Jesus as the primus resurrected means death.

Jesus the only redeemer saves and protects from eternal death and separation.

Earth's historical timeline, marred in bloody spew
from religious and political hegemony.
Wars, revolutions, religious and political
indoctrinations seal faith through fate.
The dominant hegemony whether religious or
political claims victory in blood!
Good versus evil began with the sacrifice, blood and
ends in the massacre of blood.

Holy Spirit

Holy Spirit cleanse my spirit and makes it pure.
Fire of the soul I need your purity in these days so unsure.
Dear Holy Ghost I need your serenity that is all powerful yet peaceful.
Holy fire you know my limitations, help me to comprehend Satan's subtle harm.

Holy Spirit your functions can be likened to the transmission of a neurone.
Complexities in relaying chemical-electrical impulses from cell to cell!
An urge, warning signal synchronize, borderless connects human with God the creator!
Holy Spirit omnipotent, omnipresence, omniscience purifier of the soul!

Holy Ghost all powerful never communicates through violent thrust in entering the soul.
Holy Spirit inhabits my soul, help me to remove the Laodecian cloak.
Thy source is greater in intensity than all the stars combined in the innumerable galaxies.
Heavenly Father, clouds of darkness protect man from this blinding illuminating source.

Satan's 666 Atom Smasher

Jesus compared earth's closing chapter to the days of Daniel.
King Belshazzar had a bling feast for thousand of his lords.
The pagans had defiled the golden vessels taken from the Jerusalem temple.
They praised their gods of gold, silver and wood as they became intoxicated with wine.

Belshazzar had provoked the God of Israel to wrath.
The hand of God Almighty had written Babylon's judgment and fall.
Astrologers, soothsayers, the Chaldeans could never interpret the writing on the wall.
This exposed Satan's limitation in unraveling God's designs for earth.

The Babylonians were at the height of wine and reveling.
Satan's purpose in all this was to tangelize and tarnish God the omnipotent.
The Medes and Persians strategize and attack at their final carnival.
Daniel the Jew had interpreted God's finger that decreed war and judgment.

The world today is in chaos and reveling in Rome's wormwood wine.
The hype parties and all forms of entertainment sideline the truth of the Bible.
As the global village enjoys it ultimate ball, Vatican awaits the world's final fall.

The world will awaken from it blindness with the 666 price tag system.

The Chaldeans enjoyed their last dance at Babylon's concluding hour.
The world must decide between Jesus of the Bible or the syncretism hadron's collider.
In earth's ultimate hour millions are vanity crazy and pulsating to the mamba beat.
Be sure you are covered under the blood of Jesus from Satan' 666 atom smasher!

Smooth

Smooth ... when money flows like the tide.
Smooth ... you're spending power brings esteem like the Himalaya!
Hoops! Money power creates greed and descends in disgrace.
What is the financier Bernard Madoff's fake pyramid schemes smooth criminal?

Smooth ... everything you wear is slick and is a top name brand.
Smooth ... your ego is in the expanse of space while driving or riding.
Hey! All eyes are focused and the mind quizzes "who's branding that?"
Conflict theorist decries the social inequalities between the haves and have-nots.

Smooth ... success in platinum sales and box office hits.
Ouch! The message pollutes the mind with hatred, crime and the sexually explicit.
Smooth ... entrepreneurs and officials debate and defend the hidden contents.
Gosh! Plebs and the top echelons family and society are in crisis.

Smooth ... every religion claims to have possession of the truth.
Gosh! Confusion reigns about what is politically correct or religiously correct.
Smooth ... Catholicism and many religions teach and embrace syncretism.
Jesus the truth maintains genuflection as the genuine author of life and eternal death.

Death's Big Three

Here is one of earth's greatest unsolved mysteries.
Where do people go when they die? Jesus is alive!
Many entrust their hurt to commune with mediums.
To tell the truth mediums communicate with demons, they lie.

No human souls float around as guardian angels.
They never watch over us in an endless paradise of eternal bliss.
The Bible words are plain the living praise the dead knows nothing or celebrate.
The devils inflict painful hurt and personal loss by demonic camouflage.

Recall two unseen forces, unaware to many know our moods and activities.
Demons know our temperament, unique tonality and favourite places for leisure.
Mediums channel this personal information to reassure the living.
The body dies the soul lives on, an immortal entity in another world.

Humans' souls do not become angels; it dies and the spirit returns to the Creator.
Damn what karma says humans' achieve no higher state of consciousness or nirvana
Where they are rewarded or face retribution in former life for their good or bad deeds.
In addition, the souls do not enter another human, an animal or merge with Brahman.

Evolution dictates we live the present now, no

meeting of Jesus in the sky.
Creation posits a human dies; saints are resurrected to reunite in paradise.

Satan, the demons and unrepentant humans are destroyed in the lake of fire.
Human opinions on death are pinned on the big three: karma, evolution and creation.

A Backslider's Petition

Lord help me to pray when this heart doesn't need you.
This is especially true when the enemy uses me to do his will.
Jesus how precious are those moments has my heart interacts sincerely in truth.
Lord in an age of so many hideous lights; lead me to Jesus the only genuine light.

Lord I'm tired of living a wandering life that is not purposeful.
The more I think of you sincerely it makes me want to genuflect.
Dear Jesus just one glimpse of you would inspire me to be a bit more graceful.
If daily I could read your words; prayerfully I would reflect.

Daily Satan unleashes evil in innumerable scope and depth.
Many seemed helpless and awed by the Devil's colourful deceptions.
If only their minds could be aware demons fight over our unfortified citadel.
Lord I know I'm beyond your grace and perfection without Jesus.

Majesty I am aware of my weaknesses and limitations.
I sincerely desire more of your Holy presence.
My heart craves more desires of material grandeurs and physical manifestations.
Dear Jesus only your power can help me to overcome

each worldly addiction.
Lord I am caught in the known and hidden veils of Satan's scheme.
Sometimes the glitters of the world sucks like the sin of quicksand.
Sins quicksand of worldly pleasures and views are the devil's gravity.
This unseen force pulls our hearts and minds from prayer and the truths of the Bible.

Commander Barrack

On July 4, 1776 a young unknown woman made her bold declaration.
Her thirteen colonies overwhelmed Britain under the command of George Washington.
She grew in stature when she purchased from France the province of Louisiana.
Her vastness expanded from the Atlantic to the Pacific in the gold rush to California.

Mass production through heavy industries increased her hegemony.
At a tender age her economy produced more than England, France and Germany.
Many who faced persecution or an uncertain future saw hope on her shore?
Emblems and logos were used to portray the character brand she bore.

This mighty woman proclaiming freedom for all could never tame her racial tensions.
The wall separating politics and religion never protected the blacks from the whites.
The post industrial society wounds the poor from the superrich.
Black and white contentions fume in religious splits displayed in community injustice.

Humans they say face midlife crises in their forties.
America's global reputation got battered by its 43rd president.
The 44th is a black charismatic fortified Barrack stationed at Capitol Hill.

The world ponders a professor president having world briefing with a professor pope.

America limps from the cauldron weight of wars and economic depression.
Three days she celebrates, rich and poor congregate at the Lincoln Memorial.
The president train rides to Washington, a significant retro glance with deep reflection.
Her 233rd anniversary is a foretaste of maturity for the 250th and 300th she prevails.

Capitol Hill's Barrack comforts shield and fortify a nation facing economic hardship.
Her 40th, 41st, 42nd, and 43rd leaders may have stumbled along in their duties.
The commander in chief has pitched his tent in a world facing many uncertainties.
America knows the world's watching a paradigm shift in commander Barrack leadership.

Infinity Outlast

There will be a sudden loss of desired pleasure each human must face.
Will you be able to handle the pain of loneliness that comes with dismay?
The soul battles the body to be entertained 24 hours of each day.
How will you behave when these virtual gadgets become worthless?

Our mind and spirit must be fed with the incorruptible Word which redeems.
Global calamities will create despair in souls unable to appreciate Jesus' tranquility.
The genuine revolution to rid our souls of man-made happiness must begin now.
Every soul must battle to be included in the innumerable gathering of Revelation 7.

The inauguration of Obama and other world leaders provides a calendar spectacle.
Jesus' inauguration and reign will be the phenomenon event no individual must miss.
Satan's kingdom accelerates and peaks with the institution of the 666 metonymy.
Gradually it declines and dissolves after the 1000 year reign of Jesus outlasts infinity.

Every day when I am awake I know this God given tabernacle is priceless.
Is it beneficial partying the night away until sunrise to sleep the rest of the day?
Shall I spend this day occupying my mind with fragile activities which rapidly disappear?
These 24-7 roller coaster rides will not
prepare anyone for meeting Jesus in paradise.

Calvary's Foretaste

The breach had been committed in Eden our parents could not bear.
The highest celestial being had to bore our transgressions in the flesh.
The sacrifice for sins worthlessness meant the death Jesus had to enmesh.
God's coat of skin covering Adam was fulfilled in the antitype Jesus' chosen will wear.

When he walked the street to Golgotha that day,
The Lamb of God's sacrifice on Calvary, his blood was the redemptive pay.
The Father watched the death of his son in clouds of black.
The curtains rented in Jerusalem elevating man to commune with God.

Demons and humans proclaimed oaths to put Christ to death.
Sins beginning and end he vision vividly along the path to Golgotha.
God's grace through the heavenly Lamb had bruised Satan's heel.
Satan's period of victory was replaced as Christ's head was bruised.

Calvary's foretaste meant Jesus' death and kingdom entrenched.
The immortality of the soul was Satan's guaranteed fallacious views.
Jesus the ultimate warranty had to compromise for man's disobedience.
Heaven's grace was bestowed in the veil of his crucified flesh.

Grave Miss

We the participants are caught suddenly in situations
In life's musical make up of this cast.
For some, perdition understatement is a hidden
trajectory that's going boldly too fast.
Fourteen chapters condensed within a hundred
pages questioning why her life never last.
Sadly, her passing is a grave miss;
She trekked to the river to bathe after washing her
clothes.
Fourteen chapters of her life scripted almost to
A hundred pages composed her life's prose.
The sinisters tempestuous heart left in its wake bitter
Memoirs of her life ripped apart by eerie blast.
Her mangled body appeared like devastated
vegetations uprooted,
Thrust aside where a hurricane walked.

Relatives, friends, mental apps flicker fondest
memories of her,
Rekindle nostalgic moments in jive talks.
Sincere condolences though meaningful are like
boulders
Rolling in a river that's coming down.
Rains downpour swell the volume of water flow,
Damage summing done, when water subsides within
town.
Though heartrending the loss of a loved one is,
The heart unleashes provocative outburst on
circumstances of death.
Strangling a woman to enter her paradise without
permission rips her soul,
Makes her live on the edge of the precipice.

One dashes for cover facing deadly lightning flashes,

Hopelessness clothed the soul being unaware of the abyss.
We the players dramatize life's circumstances in full-fledged laughter,
Sobbing with much regrets for losses we miss.

Miners forced, must dig rocky land for blood-diamonds,
As man usurps woman beyond her will under uncomfortable pose.
The devil-bewildered smile saturates his face,
As lustful thoughts flicker along his mental apps for how long, God knows.
He prees the victim, crouches in catlike manner,
Grasping the woman's throat, thus stopping air flow through her mouth, nose.
The domino effect of foreclosure notice signifies gloom,
So battering a plant's body to gain its colourful part-twisted dispose.
We the participants talk boldly in innocence,
Yet hideous in our demeanour before truth becomes exposed.
A huge crater reminds of a meteorite plummeting impression;
Those living within the vicinity recall its boom-tremors-hiss.
Her monumental sepulchre is engraved in our hearts',
As treasured mental apps flickers about the person via grave miss.

Her monumental sepulchre etches bittersweet memories,

Her epitaph reads gone too soon forevermore.
The rich tapestry of a persona's complexity is woven
Re-finely in serene simplicity to its core.
Her diary closes at fourteen graceful years,
Slashed within moments of a warning, goodbye
afore.
Somehow she sensed death's imminent lullaby
whispering within the surround.
The what if chorus burgeons in the environ, sadly,
Goodbye wasn't said, later she lies uprooted on the
ground.
In the fourteenth chapter, the mangled plant is
deflowered
By a few merciless beasts by the river pound.
She, a participant in life's musical trekked near
The significant crossroad learning about the world's
threshing floor.

Heavenly Father

Like inanimate objects we were lying helpless in the womb.
He sculpted us with a command through his omniscience imagination.
The heavenly Father took us up, fashioned us with his son's sword and blood.
Humanity is concept of his greatest earthly creative inspiration.
Daily after man's transgression, he took his tools to chisel down our rough edges.
Satan comprehended God's work devised schemes to tarnish what was his inspiration.
Demons were once his creative intuition carved humanity with iniquities for destruction.

He worked tirelessly to polish his personal intuition for a home in eternity.
Once he fine-tuned us a spiritual warfare continued to be battled for each soul.
When we were malleable, Jesus refined us through the scriptures and the Holy Spirit.
We understood the warmth of love through the eyes of his infinite heart.
God was our source of comfort through the protection-provision of the Passover Lamb.
Biological fathers nurture children through education for adulthood and work.
The Father sculpts soul, spirit and body to be at one accord with Jesus until he returns.

Holy Submersible

The contents of our heart Lord are pitch-black like the Marianas Trench.
We need your holy submersible to reveal the magnitude of sins in our heart.
Man always glorifies the many inventions to discover, study the universe's birth.
He will never comprehend his sinful nature until he seeks the Lord in repentance.

This genius has deciphered the genetic map,behaviour of God's known creation.
Many seem unable to fathom the continued tang lazing effects of Satan since the fall.
The Holy Spirit, your submersible was promised to renew our heart to the Bible's truth.
Sin's chameleon nature can only be cleansed by your Word, the Passover Lamb.

How can we be set free Lord from sin's nature you hate but we adore?
We may cry out to you in truth yet we embrace in love our sinful nature.
Your word Lord is the sword used to purify our body, soul and spirit.
We need your holy submersible to continue standing in the gap until Jesus returns.

When we crave the lustful desires of sin's nature your appeal becomes insignificant.
Our hearts battle daily to be victorious against the overwhelming power of sin's nature.
Thy holy submersible Lord we plead, mercy, cleanse

the hidden contents of the heart.
Our hearts belong to Jesus the master yet it gives devotion to our sinful nature.

Prayer

In prayer I communicate one to one with Jesus my special genuine friend.
Sometimes I whisper he understands the contents of my heart's intention.
With an active thought life, prayers maybe silent to escape demons interference, invasion,
When praying I request from Father unconditional love, mercy in dealing with humans.

The wise plead to God to counter petition-protection of friends from Satan's plan.
The name of Jesus and prayer are human spiritual weaponry to make demons tremble.
Whenever you are in doubt, afraid of Lucifer's agents genuflect to Jesus in prayer.
Satan's demons, human agents are scared of the proclamation "help me Jesus!"

Prayer and the human spirit bridge the gap between the spiritual, physical worlds.
We commune in physical manifestation to relay with Jesus in spiritual manifestation.
Praying to Jesus wounds, weakens demonic activities in the spiritual-physical realms.
When in danger we pray in haste, practice praying in reverence it's sincere in meaning.

In prayer request the Holy Spirit, truth's revealer, to bring out provocative secret sins.
Sins dearest to our heart should be cleansed first when praying-asking forgiveness.
Why ask forgiveness when in sincerity you are hiding those cherished forbidden ones.
Plead mercy, request for Jesus sword to sever public-private adored profane schemes.

China

She has the largest world population billions of
people like grains of sand,
Her economy, manufacturing giant produces the
good life for earth's mega corporation.
The name brand goodies for our global village are
product designed on her soil.
The inventions of kites, paper and gun powder are
her official registered trademarks.
She creates appliances, bombs, ships, airplanes and
is the target of making electric cars.
The earth ponders the amazing dam three gorges
down, the Great Wall of China.
Her muse continues in 2008, humanity awed at the
Olympic facilities, Bird Nest stadium.

She lifted millions of her own from poverty, still
millions experience economic disparity.
China's people demonstrate the teaching, philosophy
of Confucius religion.
Her brand of Buddhism an eastern religion attracts
millions to Tibet's Dalai Lama.
Needles may be an unanimous brand due to her
ancient medicinal practice acupuncture,
Dinner tables globally secular; religious festivals all
display her elegant chinaware.
Her superb dynasties governments orchestrate
grandeur dynamism of past civilization.
China today is a comprehensive Maoist-Marxist
capitalist economy of future geopolitics.

Neo-Paganism

These fools can't comprehend why the wise seek God's plan of salvation.
They are nurtured with Lucifer's initiation within the womb to the tomb.
The blue print infidels are daily conditioned with the 666 imprint implantation.
It's happening everywhere he reads; no heaven, no salvation, no God; man is god.

The sign of Jesus' second coming is closer than near.
The Bible's content is questioned by scientific methods; qualitative - quantitative findings.
Man's inquisitive mind will continue to research with no conclusion of God's blue print.
Everyone is aware that Satan's two-faced 666 systems are within the buttons resolution.

Satan's activities are infiltrated smoothly within God's milk.
Countless are trapped in deception in the midst of the Valley of Decision.
Everyone should proofread to test all materials with the Bible's teachings.
In Ezekiel God's temple in Jerusalem was polluted with demonic practices and worship.

All over the Bible God showed glimpses of his chosen people practicing neo-paganism.
Our Lord hates this Baal-Tammuz religion his children partake in.
When Christianity becomes a global business God's out while Satan's in.
Jesus needs our genuflection; it shouldn't be done to saints and other iconic images.

Chamber Of Imagery

Did you know you can reach heaven the paradise of Jesus without the narrow road?
Yes friends, heaven is within reach; it is not an eternity to look to with sin-filled load.
She isn't worried about the sinful state you are in, the church forgives sins.
Jesus knows what are your sins, these conceals you reveal to the priests in each box.

Those who have died in their sins will never enter paradise with Jesus.
The power of this church can redeem those who are not mentioned in the book of life.
The Holy Lord records her caricature features performed in her chamber of imagery.
Mother Theresa and her other saints are free in a paradise the church designed.

The die-hard may rebuff me for placing my inquisitive nose in the church's doctrines.
Oh! The transubstantiation done in the wafer-wine is another fallacious construction.
The Trent Council treaty places the Holy Sea authority on these sacraments.
This authority can release you from purgatory into heaven through indulgence.

The church's mission in all of this is to do away with Jesus' second coming.
Jesus' second judgment will wrap up Satan, the Vatican, demons and sinners in death.
Her acts of sorceries which hypnotizes men are the sins Jesus strongly condemns.

In the book of Revelation her eulogy reads lake of fire
annihilation for not repenting.

In quietude I ponder the sociology of beatification
bell tolled for her saints in heaven.
Why does this church persist, practice this ritual
dramaturgical analysis every century?
Will the bell chime in heaven when the saints
congregate before Jesus their master?
Jesus judgment verdict all actions performed in her
chamber of imagery to con men.

The Illuminati Orchestra

Global fear, panic is orchestrated by the Illuminati to
create a political new order.
Islamophobia is not the earth's greatest threat; it's the
Illuminati and a resurgent Rome.
Rome's Illuminati knows Trojan horse America leads
world order in man's global home.
The Illuminati formed America to flee Rome's
dominant Christian polity within Europe.
America's laws, pyramid seal are the Illuminati
instruments to rule earth minus Vatican.
President R freed these protocols allowing Rome to
infiltrate US government institution.
Rome the harlot in allegiance with lamblike America
ushers in Satan's 666 utopias.

Population America is programmed in behaviour to
lead the globe in these hysterias.
We are imprisoned in our social spheres in the
Illuminati games guise justice, protection.
All global alert raised alters laws with international
ones putting us in their bloody hands.
In the eleventh hour worship the penultimate test,
determines where our souls will rest.
Watch out! A global disaster-economic meltdown will
replace old with new world order.
Tomorrow the Illuminati orchestra stops the musical
food supply unless we are stamped.
Obeisance to the true savior, stomach habit will
divide humanity in Satan or Jesus camp.

Meet the Poet
Ricardo Lawton

Born at the Jubilee Hospital in Kingston, Ricardo attended the Bellfield All Age School in St. Mary. After graduating from Continuation High School, he studied at Passley Gardens Teacher's College, where he obtained a Diploma in Primary Education and started his career as a trained teacher.

Always striving for the best, Ricardo went on to study at The University of the West Indies (UWI) and graduated with his Bachelor's degree in Primary Education. He is currently employed as a teacher at the Enfield Primary and Junior High school in St. Mary, where he enjoys perfecting his craft as a teacher and exploring his desires as a writer.

Made in the USA
Columbia, SC
28 October 2024

44902275R00085